The Power Of Respect

Building Bridges to Human Peace and Human Dignity

By

Duchess Nivin ElGamal

Copyright Information

ISBN: 978-1-917601-90-0

Copyright © 2025 by Duchess Nivin ElGamal

All rights reserved.

No part of this publication may be reproduced, distributed, or transmitted in any form or by any means, including photocopying, recording, or other electronic or mechanical methods, without the prior written permission of the publisher, except in the case of brief quotations embodied in critical reviews and certain other noncommercial uses permitted by copyright law.

For permission requests, write to the author or publisher at the address provided in the contact information section of this book.

duchessoflamberton@gmail.com

Dedication

To all champions of dignity and freedom, writing a book about human rights, is a powerful way to educate and inspire change.

This book is dedicated to the unwavering pursuit of human rights, as enshrined in the Universal Declaration of Human Rights (UDHR). May the words within these pages educate, inspire, and empower individuals to strive for a world where every person can live with dignity, respect, and freedom.

Table of Contents

INTRODUCTION	5
CHAPTER 1: THE BIRTH OF THE UDHR	33
CHAPTER 2: WHY HUMAN RIGHTS MATTER TODAY	43
CHAPTER 3: HUMANITY'S UNYIELDING SPIRIT – MY PERSONAL JOURNEY	57
CHAPTER 4: STRATEGIES BEHIND THE INITIATIVES – DUCHESS NIVIN ELGAMAL'S BLUEPRINT FOR CHANGE	71
CHAPTER 5: LESSONS LEARNED – IMPLEMENTING CHANGE	81
CHAPTER 6: THE POWER OF RESPECT – A CORNERSTONE OF PEACE	90
CHAPTER 7: RESPECT AS THE PILLAR OF HUMAN RIGHTS – A GLOBAL PERSPECTIVE	99
CHAPTER 8: UNITED FOR HUMAN RIGHTS: ACTIVITIES AND ENRICHMENT FOR EMPOWERMENT	217
CHAPTER 9: COMBATTING HUMAN TRAFFICKING: A GLOBAL FIGHT AGAINST EXPLOITATION	225
CHAPTER 10: RESPECT IS EARNED, NOT BOUGHT	234
CHAPTER 11: A CALL TO ACTION	241
CHAPTER 12: REFLECTIONS AND INSPIRATIONS	248
ABOUT THE AUTHOR	252

Introduction
A Life Dedicated to Respect and Advocacy

I was born into a world of contrasts—a world where privilege existed alongside profound inequalities, where opportunity was often determined by circumstance rather than potential. From a young age, I was acutely aware of the disparities that shaped the lives of those around me, and I felt a deep responsibility to address them.
This sense of purpose became the cornerstone of my life's work: advocating for human rights and promoting respect as a universal value.

Throughout my journey, I have experienced joy and hardship, triumph and failure. These experiences have shaped me into the person I am today—a passionate advocate, a resilient leader, and a firm believer in the transformative power of respect.

The Power of Respect

Early Life: Seeds of Empathy
I was raised in an environment that exposed me to the complexities of human experience. While I was fortunate to have access to education and opportunities, I often witnessed the struggles of those less privileged. These early encounters sparked a desire to make a difference, though I didn't yet know how I would channel that passion.

One defining moment from my childhood remains vivid in my memory. During a visit to a bustling marketplace, I saw a boy no older than myself working tirelessly under the scorching sun. The disparity between our lives struck me deeply. I couldn't ignore the injustice of it, and it was then that I began to understand the importance of advocating for those whose voices are unheard.

Challenges and Growth
Life has not always been kind. Like everyone, I have faced my share of challenges—some personal, others professional. My journey has been marked by public scrutiny, moments of self-doubt, and hard lessons learned.

One of the most difficult periods in my life came when my personal relationships were thrust into the public eye. The media's harsh judgment was relentless, and I often felt isolated. However, these experiences taught me resilience and empathy. They reminded me that everyone deserves respect, even when they are at their most vulnerable.

I have also made mistakes along the way, but each one has been a teacher. They have shown me the importance of listening, adapting, and remaining true to my values. Through these challenges, I discovered the strength to transform pain into purpose.

A Commitment to Advocacy
My work as an advocate has taken me to some of the world's most vulnerable communities—refugee camps, conflict zones, and underserved neighborhoods. Each place has deepened my understanding of humanity's resilience and the importance of respect in fostering hope and healing.

I have dedicated my efforts to empowering women and girls, supporting displaced families, and promoting mental health. These initiatives are not just about providing aid; they are about restoring dignity and creating opportunities for individuals to thrive. One of my proudest moments came when I saw a group of young girls, once denied education, stand on a stage and share their dreams for the future. Their courage reminded me why this work matters.

The Power of Respect

The Role of Respect in My Life
Respect is not just a value I advocate for—it is a principle I strive to live by. Whether engaging with global leaders or listening to the stories of displaced individuals, I have learned that respect is the foundation of trust, understanding, and peace.

In every interaction, I try to embody the belief that every person has inherent worth. This philosophy has guided my work and shaped the initiatives I have led, from creating safe learning spaces for children, to promoting cross-cultural dialogue in divided communities.

Why I Wrote This Book
"The Power of Respect: Building Bridges to Peace and Human Dignity" is a reflection of my journey and the lessons I have learned along the way. It is a call to action for individuals, families, and leaders to embrace respect as the foundation of a more equitable and peaceful world.

This book is not just my story—it is the story of every person I have met who has inspired me to keep fighting for justice and dignity. It is for the young girl in Kabul who dreams of a better future, the refugee who rebuilds his life from nothing, and the countless individuals who remind us that respect has the power to transform lives.

A Message of Hope
As I continue my journey, I remain committed to building bridges of understanding, fostering dignity, and promoting peace. I invite you to join me in this mission. Together, we can create a world where respect is not just an ideal but a lived reality—one that honors the universal principles of human rights and ensures a brighter future for generations to come.

Autobiography: Duchess Nivin ElGamal – The Power of Respect

The Power of Respect

Anecdotes from Early Life: Seeds of Advocacy

1. The Market Encounter
As a child, I once accompanied my mother to a local market. Among the bustling stalls, I noticed a girl my age sitting on the ground, selling vegetables while scribbling on a torn piece of paper with a broken pencil. She was trying to do her homework while helping her family. I couldn't stop thinking about her that night and asked my mother why some children had to work instead of going to school. That experience ignited my desire to address educational inequality.

2. Learning Compassion from My Grandfather and Grandmother
My grandparents once told me, *"You measure the greatness of a person by how they treat someone who can do nothing for them."* Those words have stayed with me throughout my life, shaping how I view kindness and humanity. I still vividly remember my first months in London, starting on July 31, 2001. I had just arrived from Egypt, leaving everything behind to begin a new life in the UK. By November, I had run out of money and found myself wandering the unfamiliar streets,

The Power of Respect

shivering in the biting cold. As I walked, I noticed a homeless woman sitting on the pavement. Without hesitation, I took off my only coat and gave it to her. It was an impulsive act of compassion, even though I knew it meant braving the freezing night without it. In that moment, standing there coatless, I not only felt the bitter chill of the air but also the profound weight of her circumstances—unfair, inescapable, and deeply isolating.

The next day, something extraordinary happened. I found a job, and my employer offered me an advance on my wages. With that money, I bought a secondhand coat, and I remember feeling a joy that was almost indescribable. It wasn't just the relief of having warmth again—it was the overwhelming sense that my selflessness had been rewarded, as though God had recognized and blessed that small, kind gesture.

That moment taught me that compassion doesn't have to be grand or calculated. It begins with small, selfless acts, often made in moments when you yourself may not have much to give. It's those seemingly insignificant choices that truly define us and, in the end, bring us closer to our own humanity.

The Power of Respect

Anecdotes from Challenges: Resilience in the Face of Adversity

3. The Weight of Public Scrutiny

During a particularly challenging period in my life, I read a scathing article about myself that was riddled with inaccuracies and that I converted from my religion. I felt anger and humiliation, but instead of reacting, I channeled my energy into writing an op-ed about the importance of understanding and respecting others' personal struggles. That piece resonated with many, turning my pain into a platform for advocacy.

4. A Lesson in Forgiveness

Someone close to me betrayed my trust, leaving me deeply hurt. For weeks, I wrestled with anger and resentment, unsure how to move forward. But eventually, I turned to God for guidance and decided to confront the situation with honesty and forgiveness. It wasn't easy, but through prayer and faith, I found the strength to let go of my pain. In choosing forgiveness, I discovered a profound peace within myself—a peace that only God can provide.

This experience taught me that forgiveness is part of God's plan for healing. If I cannot forgive someone else, how can I stand before God and ask for His forgiveness? Forgiveness isn't about condoning the hurt but following God's example of grace and mercy. It's a way to free ourselves from the chains of bitterness and reflect the love of God, who forgives us despite our own imperfections. By forgiving others, I honor God's teachings and recognize that His grace is greater than any pain I've endured.

Anecdotes from Advocacy: The Impact of Respect

5. **The School That Wasn't There**
During a visit to a rural community, I met a group of children who walked miles to reach a school that didn't even have proper classrooms. Instead of desks, they sat on the floor under a tree. I was deeply moved and worked with local leaders to build a fully equipped school. Returning a year later to see the children thriving was one of the most fulfilling moments of my life.

6. **The Refugee Who Taught Me Hope**
In a refugee camp, I met a man named Adam, who had fled war with nothing but his family. Despite his losses, he had started a small vegetable garden to feed his neighbors. Adam said, "When everything is taken from you, respect, education and hope are the only things you have left." His resilience and dignity inspired me to launch a gardening initiative in the

camp, transforming barren spaces into flourishing community gardens.

Anecdotes from Leadership: Lessons in Respect

7. Listening to the Quietest Voice
During a meeting with my team, I noticed a junior member hesitating to share her idea. I encouraged her to speak, and her suggestion turned out to be the solution we needed for a major challenge. That moment reminded me of the importance of respecting and valuing every voice, no matter how quiet, and assured to make everyone feel self worth and confident about themselves.

8. A Lesson in Cultural Sensitivity
In a community project, I initially overlooked a local tradition while designing an initiative. A community elder gently pointed it out, and I immediately adapted the program to honor their customs. That experience deepened my understanding of cultural respect as a cornerstone of effective leadership.

Anecdotes from Education: Transforming Lives

9. The Girl Who Found Her Voice

At school, I was bullied by a close friend because of my voice, which they cruelly called a "bird voice." Their words cut deeply, leaving me ashamed and traumatized. From that point on, I avoided speaking whenever I could. My voice felt like a burden, something I had to hide. I stopped raising my hand in class, avoided participating in discussions, and withdrew from any situation where my voice might be heard. Even as I grew older, this fear stayed with me. When I was handed a microphone at events, I would freeze, panic rising in my chest, and I'd turn down the opportunity. My voice was blocked inside me, locked away by the fear of judgment. For years, I felt powerless, as though I didn't deserve to be heard.

Then later in life I met Charlotte. She was a quiet girl in my community who rarely spoke, always sitting at the back of the room. One day, I mustered the courage to ask her why she stayed so silent. She looked at me and said something that struck a deep chord: "No one listens to me." Her words mirrored my own unspoken fears, and I realized how much I wanted to help her overcome what I myself had struggled with for so long.

The Power of Respect

Determined to make a difference, I spoke to the head of the group and encouraged them to create safe and supportive opportunities for Charlotte to participate. Slowly but surely, she began to find her voice. First, she answered questions seminars. Then she joined zoom group discussions. By the end of the year, Charlotte was leading debates, captivating us all with her ideas, and inspiring those around her. Watching her transformation felt like watching a flower bloom. Her courage reignited something in me—a desire to reclaim my own voice.

Charlotte's journey became my wake-up call. If she could overcome her fears and speak her truth, then why couldn't I? I began to reflect on why voice and self-expression mattered so much. Our voices are not just tools for communication; they are the essence of who we are. They hold our stories, our truths, and our power. To speak is to claim our right to exist, to connect, and to influence the world around us. Public speaking, I came to understand, is not just about standing on a stage—it is about sharing ideas, inspiring change, and embracing the freedom to be ourselves.

Charlotte's courage reminded me that my voice, no matter how it sounded, had value. Slowly, I began to confront my fear. I started small—sharing my

The Power of Respect

thoughts in conversations, speaking up in meetings, and eventually accepting the microphone when it was handed to me. Each time I spoke, it felt like breaking through a barrier I had built long ago. Over time, I found not only my voice but also the freedom and confidence to use it.

Looking back, I realize that our voices are our most powerful tools for change. The ability to speak, to explain, and to connect is a gift we should never take for granted. The power of public speaking lies in its ability to bridge divides, inspire action, and affirm our shared humanity. And the freedom of speech is not just a right—it is a responsibility to ensure that no one feels silenced, whether by others or by their own fears.

Charlotte gave me a gift far greater than I ever gave her. She reminded me that our voices matter, no matter how small or different they may seem, and that the world needs to hear them. Her transformation was the spark that reignited mine, and for that, I will always be grateful.

For example, during a court hearing, I found myself wondering why people always had to explain themselves in such great detail. Then it became clear to me: the power of providing clear and accurate information is essential for the judge to fully

The Power of Respect

understand the case and deliver a fair judgment based on the truth. Without proper explanation, how could the person in front of us—whether a judge, friend, or anyone—truly understand what happened or the surrounding circumstances?

This applies to everyday life as well. Take a simple example: if I'm upset with my friend, she won't automatically know how I feel if I act normal around her. Unless I explain my feelings, she'll remain unaware of the problem, and we won't resolve it. This is how we set boundaries in relationships—by using our words to let others know when they've crossed a line or hurt us. Without speaking up, we risk being misunderstood or allowing people to unintentionally harm us.

Our voice is a powerful tool, not only to express ourselves but also to create understanding, build connections, and set expectations. Without explanation, no one can fully grasp our perspective, and without our voice, we lose the opportunity to shape the way others treat us or interpret our experiences. That's why the ability to speak and explain is so important—it's the foundation of understanding, fairness, and healthy relationships.

10. The Letter from a Student

I once received a handwritten letter from a student at the university where my father own, and its words have stayed with me ever since. The student wrote, "Thank you for believing in us. Because of this university, I know I can become a leader and help my community." It was a simple message, yet profoundly moving. In that moment, I was reminded of the transformative power of education—not just as a tool for personal success, but as a means to inspire and empower individuals to uplift entire communities.

That letter reinforced why this work matters so much. Education is not merely about imparting knowledge; it is about planting the seeds of confidence, resilience, and vision. By believing in students, by giving them the tools and support they need, we help them see beyond their current circumstances and imagine what is possible. For many students, especially those from underserved communities, education is not just an opportunity—it's a lifeline. It provides them with the skills to break cycles of poverty, the confidence to lead, and the courage to create change.

The letter also reminded me of the ripple effect of investing in others. When a student believes they can lead, they don't just transform their own lives; they become a beacon for others in their community, proving that progress is possible. It is a legacy of hope and change that extends far beyond the walls of the university.

It's moments like these that reaffirm the importance of this work and the responsibility we have to nurture the next generation of leaders. By believing in their potential, we contribute to something far greater than ourselves—a brighter, more equitable future for all.#

Anecdotes from Global Work: Respect across Borders

11. The Shared Meal

At an international conference, participants from conflicting regions were invited to a cultural dinner—a space intentionally created to foster connection beyond political tensions. The long banquet table was adorned with vibrant dishes from around the world: warm, fragrant biryanis, tender slow-cooked lamb tagine, buttery naan, freshly grilled kebabs, and colorful platters of hummus, tabbouleh, and dolmas. For dessert, there were delicate baklava dripping with honey and creamy tiramisu, accompanied by steaming cups of mint tea and rich Turkish coffee.

At first, the atmosphere was stiff. Participants from opposing sides of a conflict kept to themselves,

The Power of Respect

avoiding eye contact. But as the dishes were served and the aromas filled the room, something began to shift. I watched as two delegates, who had never spoken to each other before, hesitated but then reached for the same platter of stuffed grape leaves. They exchanged a polite smile, and it was the first crack in the wall of silence between them.

As the evening unfolded, they began sharing stories about their childhoods, sparked by the food on their plates. One delegate reminisced about how his grandmother made lamb tagine on special occasions, while the other recalled the communal feasts of his village. Their voices grew softer, their gestures more animated, and before long, the tension between them had melted away. By the end of the night, they were laughing and talking about future collaborations as though they'd known each other for years.

This experience reminded me of the universal power of food to bring people together. Sharing a meal goes beyond nourishment—it's a gesture of hospitality, a way of saying, "I see you, and I welcome you." In the presence of good food, walls come down.

People feel softened, more comfortable, and open to conversation. Food carries culture, memory, and emotion, and when it is shared, it creates a neutral ground where even those with opposing views can connect as human beings. Breaking bread together is an act of trust. It invites dialogue and fosters a sense of safety, even in the aftermath of conflict. In this instance, the cultural dinner transformed a formal conference into a space for empathy and understanding. It showed me that, sometimes, the simplest acts—like sharing a delicious meal—can lead to profound breakthroughs. It's a reminder that even in the most divided settings, common ground can be found, one bite at a time.

12. **The Woman Who Changed the Room**
At a United Nations panel, a woman named Tahani from Yemen shared her harrowing story of survival during years of conflict and displacement. Tahani described how she and her husband were forced to move repeatedly due to the war, enduring extreme poverty and the devastating loss of their first child due to lack of medical care. Despite these hardships, she discovered a way to rebuild her life through a resilience program supported by the International Organization for Migration (IOM). Tahani learned skills in crafting handmade accessories, which not only provided an income but also gave her a renewed sense of purpose and confidence. Her journey from despair to empowerment moved the audience deeply, earning her a standing ovation. After the panel, Tahani

The Power of Respect

confided, "I thought my story didn't matter, but today, I see how much power it holds." Her courage highlighted the importance of creating spaces where individuals can share their experiences, fostering understanding and collective action. Stories like hers remind us of the resilience of the human spirit and the transformative power of giving people the tools and support to reclaim their lives.

This moment underscores how storytelling—whether in formal panels or personal conversations—bridges divides and inspires change. It also demonstrates the value of empowering women, particularly in conflict zones, to become active contributors to their communities and decision-making processes, showcasing how personal resilience can lead to collective progress. Her words moved the entire room to a standing ovation.

Anecdotes from the Power of Respect

13. Respecting Nature
In 2001, while planting trees with a group of children, one boy said something that changed my perspective forever: *"These trees will grow because we respected the land."* His words were simple, yet profound, and they resonated deeply with me. They weren't just

The Power of Respect

about planting trees—they carried a message of harmony, humility, and the interconnectedness of humanity and nature. That moment stayed with me, igniting a desire to honor the land and its sacred role in sustaining life.

Since that day, inspired by that boy's words, I have made it my mission to plant olive trees in every country I visit. To me, the olive tree is more than just a plant—it is a symbol of peace, resilience, and unity. Its deep roots and enduring nature reflect the kind of harmony I wish to cultivate in the world. Each tree I plant carries the hope that it will one day bear fruit, provide shade, or stand as a testament to the values of respect and sustainability.

This mission also reminds me of the wisdom of the late Sheikh Zayed Al Nahyan of UAE, the visionary leader of the UAE. Sheikh Zayed demonstrated his unwavering commitment to the environment through countless acts of conservation. One of his most profound lessons was his decision to protect trees, famously saying that trees symbolize life, growth, and sustainability. He understood that preserving the environment wasn't just an ecological act but a moral one—a promise to future generations.

The Power of Respect

Sheikh Zayed's leadership embodied a respect for the land and its resources, teaching us that progress should never come at the expense of nature. His vision of leadership was grounded in humility and selflessness, believing that to serve people, one must also safeguard the world they inhabit. His life and actions inspire me to see environmental stewardship not just as a responsibility, but as an act of love and respect for humanity.

As I plant each olive tree, I am reminded of the interconnectedness of all living things. The act of planting isn't just about the physical act of digging a hole and placing a sapling—it's about hope, renewal, and the belief that small actions can create ripples of change. Every tree stands as a reminder that respect for the environment is deeply tied to respect for each other and the future we wish to create.

Sheikh Zayed's teachings and the words of that young boy continue to guide me. Together, they remind me that greatness lies not in grand gestures, but in thoughtful actions that honor both the earth and its people. The trees I plant are my tribute to their wisdom—a living legacy of hope and respect for generations to come.

The Power of Respect

14. The Power of a Smile
During a tense negotiation, I greeted a skeptical participant with a warm smile and a genuine compliment. That simple gesture softened the atmosphere and allowed us to find common ground.

15. The Handshake That Ended a Feud
At a reconciliation meeting between two communities, a simple handshake between their leaders marked the end of decades of hostility. That handshake was a testament to the power of mutual respect.

I am incorporating personal anecdotes from my Instagram posts to enrich this autobiography, providing readers with authentic insights into my experiences and advocacy work. Here are several anecdotes inspired by my Instagram content: **@duchess_nivin_elgamal_official**

1. Championing Change in the UK
In a recent Instagram post, I expressed my support for the Labour Party, emphasizing the need for change in the UK's political landscape. I stated: "Are you ready for change, UK? Vote Labour on July 4th! #labour 🏴 "[Piokok]

The Power of Respect

(https://www.piokok.com/profile/duchess_nivin_elgamal_official/?utm_source=))

This post reflects my commitment to political engagement and my belief in the power of collective action to bring about societal improvements.

2. Embracing True Colors

I shared a personal revelation about aligning with my true self, mentioning my affinity for the color red and my decision to support the Labour Party. I wrote:

"When destiny pushed me to the right path, I finally embraced my true colors.

I've loved red since I was born; most of my cars are red, and my brand Duchess Prestige is red." (https://www.piokok.com/profile/duchess_nivin_elgamal_official/?utm_source=)

This anecdote illustrates my journey toward authenticity and the importance of staying true to one's beliefs and passions.

Creating my own unique red shade involves a combination of experimentation and precision. Here's a step-by-step guide to how I created a customized red color for Duchess Prestige.

The Power of Respect

1. Define My Vision
Decide what kind of red I wanted:
Undertones: Cool (blueish) or warm (orangey)?
Shade: Bright, deep, muted, or pastel?
Finish: Matte, glossy, metallic, or shimmery?
Pigments: Start with primary colors (red, yellow, blue) and white/black for adjustments. Red oxide, carmine, crimson, scarlet, or synthetic red pigments are good bases.

2. Tools
Mixing palette or bowls.
Measuring spoons or a scale for precision.
Spatula or mixing tool.

3. Start with a Base Red
Used a pre-existing red pigment & blend yellow and magenta to form a starting red.
Tested the base shade on a surface similar to my final application.

4. Adjust Undertones
Warm Undertones: Small amounts of yellow or orange were added to create a welcoming and uplifting effect.
Cool Undertones: Small amounts of blue or purple were introduced for a calm and serene feel.

The Power of Respect

After experimenting with both options, I decided to go for warm undertones. I was searching for a color that could convey joy, pleasure, and respect, while also evoking a cozy and comfortable atmosphere. Warm tones create a sense of acceptance and belonging, which aligns perfectly with the emotions I wanted to evoke.

5. Adjust Brightness or Depth

To Brighten: Add white, but sparingly to avoid creating a pink tone.

To Deepen: Add black for a darker tone or a hint of blue for a richer, wine-like red.

Faced with a decision to either brighten or deepen the color, I ultimately chose to brighten it, giving it a more vibrant and energetic feel. To enhance its impact, I added a black color right next to it, shaped into flowing waves. This choice was intentional—to evoke the feeling of the sea and its profound depths, creating a striking contrast that made the bright red even more dynamic and alive. The interplay between the bright red and the deep black captured both vitality and depth, embodying a sense of movement and emotion, much like the rhythm of ocean waves.

Out of respect for my brand and its identity, I decided to choose a bold and standout color. I wanted something that could command attention and reflect confidence, aligning with the values of strength and individuality. My decision was inspired by a personal experience: whenever I go to purchase cosmetic products, I often find shelves dominated by similar shades of blue, pink, and white. In moments when I'm in a rush—like before an important meeting—it's hard to quickly identify a product among such repetitive and understated tones.

This frustration drove my choice to go bold. I wanted my brand's color to not only stand out but to make a statement—ensuring it would be easily recognizable and leave a lasting impression. Bold colors symbolize respect for the consumer's time and experience, offering them something distinct and easy to locate, even in a hurry. It's not just about standing out; it's about delivering respect through thoughtful design and usability.

3. Advocating for Women's Empowerment

During International Women's Month, I was honored for my contributions to women's rights and empowerment. In my acceptance speech, I dedicated the award to my son and emphasized the significance of perseverance. I stated:

"I wanted to be an extraordinary woman, an example in my job and my life for other single women. I wanted to be an ideal,

extraordinary mother, fulfilling all my son's demands—maintaining his upbringing in the Arab traditions and the Islamic religion."

[London Business Magazine] (https://londonbusinessmagazine.com/duchess-nivin-el-gamal-of-lamberton-honored-for-outstanding-womens-achievement/?utm_source=)

4. Judging Mr. England Competition

As a judge for the Mr. England competition, I witnessed Lance Corporal Manuel Alcantara Turner's journey to victory. I remarked:

"He truly embodies everything we look for in a Mr. England – a perfect combination of ambition, responsibility, dignity, and respect."

[Forces-News] (https://www.forcesnews.com/services/army/bearskin-hat-mr-england-sash-coldstream-guard-wins-beauty-pageant?utm_source=))

My involvement in this event underscores my commitment to recognizing and promoting individuals who exemplify positive values and leadership.

5. **Overcoming Personal Adversity**

I have openly shared my personal journey, including challenges in my relationships and legal battles. Reflecting on these experiences, I mentioned:

"My life wasn't a sad story; it was a testament to the power of perseverance and the beauty of finding light in the darkest of times."

[Piokok](https://www.piokok.com/profile/duchess_nivin_elgamal_official/?utm_source=))

This narrative showcases my resilience and determination to transform adversity into opportunities for growth and advocacy. These anecdotes, drawn from my Instagram posts, provide a glimpse into my multifaceted life as a philanthropist, advocate, and mother, illustrate the depth of my commitment to promoting respect, dignity, and positive change in society.

For more insights and updates on my advocacy work, readers can follow my Instagram account: [@duchess_nivin_elgamal_official]
(https://www.instagram.com/duchess_nivin_elgamal_official/).

The Power of Respect

Chapter 1: The Birth of the UDHR

Introduction: A World in Ashes

The streets of Berlin in 1945 were unrecognizable, strewn with rubble and ash. Buildings that once stood as symbols of progress and culture were now hollow shells, their windows blown out like empty, accusing eyes. Across Europe, families sifted through debris in search of loved ones or belongings, while in Asia, the cities of Hiroshima and Nagasaki bore scars of devastation unimaginable in human history.

The war had left a scar not just on the land but on the collective conscience of humanity. In the ruins of the Dachau concentration camp, Allied soldiers uncovered a horror that words struggled to describe—piles of emaciated corpses, gas chambers stained with the residues of Zyklon B, and the stench of death that lingered long after the camp was liberated.

The world had reached its nadir. The brutality of World War II had revealed the darkest depths of human cruelty, and with it came an urgent question:

how could such atrocities be prevented in the future? The global community knew that treaties and political agreements alone were insufficient. What was needed was a framework of principles that transcended borders, a universal acknowledgment of the inherent dignity of every human being.

It was from this rubble—both literal and moral—that the Universal Declaration of Human Rights (UDHR) emerged, a beacon of hope for a weary world.

The Road to the UDHR
The creation of the United Nations in 1945 was itself an act of defiance against despair. Conceived in San Francisco by 51 founding nations, the UN was not just a political body; it was a symbol of humanity's commitment to peace and cooperation. Among its most ambitious goals was the establishment of a document that would enshrine the rights of every individual, a moral guide for the world to follow.

Eleanor Roosevelt: A Relentless Advocate
At the helm of this monumental task was Eleanor Roosevelt, one of the most influential women of her time. Eleanor was no stranger to adversity. As the wife of President Franklin D. Roosevelt, she had witnessed the Great Depression's crushing toll on American families. As a First Lady, she had traveled extensively,

seeing firsthand the plight of the disenfranchised. Her empathy for the marginalized fueled her commitment to human rights. She accepted the role of chairperson for the UN Commission on Human Rights with characteristic humility and determination. In her opening address to the commission, she declared:

"We stand today at the threshold of a great event, both in the life of the United Nations and in the life of mankind. This declaration may well become the international Magna Carta for all men everywhere."

Roosevelt's leadership was instrumental in guiding the commission through the many obstacles that lay ahead. She possessed a rare combination of pragmatism and idealism, which allowed her to mediate between opposing viewpoints while keeping the ultimate goal in sight.

René Cassin: The Architect of Justice

René Cassin, a French jurist and Holocaust survivor, brought his legal expertise and personal experiences to the drafting table. Cassin had lost 29 members of his family to Nazi atrocities, and the horrors of the Holocaust were etched into his memory. He approached the task with a sense of urgency, knowing that the world needed a legal and moral framework to prevent such crimes from happening again. Cassin's draft of the UDHR drew heavily from the French Declaration of the Rights of Man and the Citizen, blending its revolutionary ideals with modern principles of equality and justice.

It was Cassin who suggested organizing the declaration into 30 succinct articles, each addressing a fundamental aspect of human dignity. His ability to translate lofty ideals into practical language earned him the nickname " The architect of the UDHR"

A Global Effort

The commission's members represented a wide array of cultural, philosophical, and political perspectives. Charles Malik of Lebanon, a philosopher and diplomat, brought a deep understanding of ethics and individual freedom. Peng Chun Chang of China, a Confucian scholar, emphasized the importance of harmony and collective rights. Together, these individuals embodied the diversity of the global community, ensuring that the declaration would resonate across cultures.

Their debates were intense and often contentious. Should the declaration prioritize individual rights or collective responsibilities? How could it address both civil liberties and socioeconomic equality? Each delegate brought their unique perspective to the table, resulting in a document that was as much a product of negotiation as it was of vision.

The Drafting Process

The drafting of the Universal Declaration of Human Rights (UDHR) was a process as rigorous as it was inspiring. With 18 members representing a diverse set of nations, cultures, and philosophies, the Commission on Human Rights became a microcosm of the world it aimed to serve. The debates were often passionate, occasionally combative, and always driven by a shared sense of purpose: to create a document that would uphold the dignity of every human being.

Debates Across Cultures and Ideologies

From the very beginning, the commission grappled with one fundamental question: What does it mean to be human? This question shaped every discussion, and the answers were as varied as the delegates themselves.

The East and West Divide

The ideological divide between the capitalist West and the communist East was stark. Western nations, led by the United States and the United Kingdom, emphasized individual freedoms, such as freedom of speech, religion, and the press. They believed these rights were the foundation of democracy and a bulwark against tyranny. The Soviet Union, on the other hand, argued that individual rights were meaningless without the guarantee of economic and social rights. They insisted on the inclusion of provisions for the right to work, education, and healthcare, which they viewed as essential for achieving true equality.

The debates were fierce. Charles Malik of Lebanon, a staunch advocate of civil liberties, clashed with Soviet representatives who accused the West of prioritizing individualism at the expense of social welfare. Eleanor Roosevelt acted as a mediator, urging the delegates to find common ground.

Ultimately, the commission chose to include both sets of rights, creating a declaration that recognized the importance of freedom and equality in all its dimensions. This compromise was a testament to the commission's determination to create a truly universal document.

Religious and Philosophical Influences
The diversity of the commission extended beyond politics. Delegates brought with them a rich tapestry of religious and philosophical traditions that shaped their perspectives on human rights.

- Western Liberalism: The Enlightenment ideals of individual liberty and reason were championed by Western delegates like René Cassin, who drew inspiration from the French Revolution's Declaration of the Rights of Man and the Citizen.
- Eastern Philosophy: Peng Chun Chang emphasized the Confucian values of harmony, respect, and collective responsibility. He argued that rights should not only protect individuals but also promote social cohesion.
- Post-Colonial Perspectives: Delegates from newly independent nations, such as India and Pakistan, stressed the importance of self-determination and the rights of oppressed peoples. Hansa Mehta of India, a staunch advocate for women's rights, ensured that the declaration used gender-inclusive language.

These philosophical influences enriched the drafting process, ensuring that the UDHR reflected the aspirations of a global community rather than a single ideology.

Milestones in the Drafting Process
The journey from concept to adoption was marked by several key milestones, each representing a step closer

to the realization of a universal framework for human rights.

The Secretariat Draft
The first draft of the UDHR was prepared by John Humphrey, a Canadian law professor and director of the UN's Division of Human Rights. His 400-page document was an exhaustive compilation of rights from existing declarations, constitutions, and international treaties.

Humphrey's draft served as a starting point for the commission's deliberations. René Cassin took the lead in distilling its content into a more concise and cohesive document, which he presented to the commission in 1947.

The Lake Success Meetings
In the spring of 1948, the commission convened at Lake Success, New York, for a series of intensive meetings. These sessions were marked by heated debates over language, priorities, and the scope of the declaration.

One of the most contentious issues was the question of enforcement. Some delegates argued for a binding treaty that would hold nations accountable for violations, while others preferred a non-binding declaration that could serve as a moral guide. In the end, the latter approach prevailed, as it was seen as more feasible in a world still deeply divided.

The Third Committee Review
In the fall of 1948, the draft declaration was submitted to the UN General Assembly's Third Committee, which was responsible for social, humanitarian, and cultural issues. The committee conducted a line-by-line review of the text, with delegates proposing amendments and debating every word.

One notable moment occurred when Hansa Mehta successfully argued for the phrase "all men are created equal" to be replaced with "all human beings are born free and equal." This change reflected a commitment to gender equality and marked a significant victory for women's rights advocates.

Final Drafting in Paris
By December 1948, the final draft of the UDHR was ready for adoption. The commission gathered at the Palais de Chaillot in Paris, a city still recovering from the scars of war. The atmosphere was tense but hopeful as delegates prepared to vote on what Eleanor Roosevelt called "a declaration of the rights of man in the 20th century."

The Power of Respect

A Declaration for All Humanity

The adoption of the UDHR on December 10, 1948, was a triumph of diplomacy and human solidarity. As the roll call proceeded, 48 nations voted in favor of the declaration. While eight countries abstained, citing political or cultural concerns, no nation voted against it—a remarkable achievement in a world still reeling from division and conflict.

In the words of René Cassin, the UDHR was "the first document of international law to affirm the dignity of every human being." It was not perfect, nor was it universally accepted, but it was a beginning—a shared promise to protect and promote the rights of all people.

The Power of Respect

Chapter 2: Why Human Rights Matter Today

The Universal Declaration of Human Rights (UDHR) is more than just a historical artifact; it is a living document that continues to shape the lives of billions of people around the world. Its principles have transcended the moment of their creation, finding relevance in the struggles for justice, equality, and freedom that define our time.

Yet, despite its universal aspirations, the ideals enshrined in the UDHR remain far from realized. Human trafficking, systemic racism, political oppression, and inequality are daily realities for countless individuals.

This chapter explores why the UDHR still matters today by examining its role in addressing contemporary challenges, inspiring global movements, and providing a framework for justice and accountability.

The Power of Respect

The Enduring Relevance of the UDHR
More than seven decades after its adoption, the UDHR remains a touchstone for human rights advocates, policymakers, and ordinary citizens. But why does a document drafted in the aftermath of World War II still resonate in today's complex, interconnected world?

A Universal Moral Compass
At its core, the UDHR provides a universal language of dignity and respect. It affirms that every person, regardless of their race, gender, nationality, or socioeconomic status, is entitled to fundamental rights. This simple yet profound idea has inspired countless individuals and movements.

For example, Article 1's declaration that "all human beings are born free and equal in dignity and rights" has been a rallying cry for marginalized communities seeking justice. From women's rights advocates in the 1960s till now, the UDHR has provided a moral foundation for challenging discrimination and inequality.

A Framework for Accountability
The UDHR has also served as the basis for legally binding treaties, such as the International Covenant on Civil and Political Rights (ICCPR) and the

The Power of Respect

International Covenant on Economic, Social and Cultural Rights (ICESCR). Together, these treaties form the International Bill of Human Rights, providing mechanisms to hold states accountable for violations.

In cases of genocide, war crimes, and crimes against humanity, the UDHR has been a guiding light for international justice. The establishment of tribunals, such as those for Rwanda and the former Yugoslavia, and the creation of the International Criminal Court (ICC) owe much to the declaration's principles.

Contemporary Challenges to Human Rights
Despite its achievements, the UDHR faces significant challenges in a world that remains deeply divided by conflict, inequality, and oppression.

Rising Authoritarianism
In recent years, the rise of authoritarian regimes has threatened the progress made in advancing human rights. Leaders in countries such as North Korea, Myanmar, and Belarus have flouted international norms, suppressing dissent, silencing journalists, and violating the rights of their citizens.

The UDHR's emphasis on freedom of expression (Article 19) and the right to participate in government

(Article 21) is more relevant than ever in the face of such repression. Civil society groups and international organizations continue to use the declaration as a tool to expose abuses and advocate for change.

Economic Inequality
Economic disparities remain a significant barrier to realizing human rights for all. While the UDHR recognizes the right to work (Article 23) and the right to an adequate standard of living (Article 25), billions of people live in poverty, lacking access to education, healthcare, and basic necessities.

The COVID-19 pandemic exacerbated these inequalities, disproportionately affecting vulnerable populations. The global response to the crisis highlighted both the importance of human rights and the challenges of ensuring their protection in times of emergency.

Technology and Privacy
The digital age has brought new opportunities and challenges for human rights. While technology has empowered movements for justice and democracy, it has also been used to surveil, manipulate, and oppress. The right to privacy (Article 12) is under threat in an era of mass data collection and cyber surveillance. Governments and corporations alike have been

accused of infringing on individuals' rights through invasive technologies.

Inspiring Global Movements
One of the most powerful legacies of the UDHR is its ability to inspire grassroots movements for change.

Civil Rights Movements
The Civil Rights Movement in the United States drew heavily on the language and principles of the UDHR. Leaders like Martin Luther King Jr. and Malcolm X framed their struggles for racial equality as part of a broader human rights movement, connecting their cause to global efforts for justice.

Women's Rights
The feminist movement has also found inspiration in the UDHR. Articles affirming equality and non-discrimination have been instrumental in advocating for gender equality, from securing women's right to vote to combating gender-based violence.

Youth and Climate Activism
In recent years, youth-led movements have emerged as powerful advocates for human rights, particularly in the context of climate change. Activists like Greta Thunberg have argued that environmental

degradation is a violation of fundamental rights, such as the right to life and the right to health.

The UDHR in Action: Stories of Change
The impact of the UDHR can best be understood through the stories of individuals and communities who have used it to fight for justice.

Nelson Mandela and the Anti-Apartheid Struggle
Nelson Mandela often cited the UDHR as a source of inspiration during his fight against apartheid in South Africa. The declaration's affirmation of equality and freedom became a rallying cry for those seeking to dismantle institutionalized racism.

Malala Yousafzai and the Right to Education
Malala Yousafzai's advocacy for girls' education in Pakistan is another example of the UDHR's enduring relevance. Her struggle reflects the principles of Article 26, which recognizes the right to education as fundamental to human dignity.

A Call to Action
The UDHR reminds us that human rights are not abstract ideals but lived realities. They are the difference between freedom and oppression, opportunity and exclusion, life and death.

The Power of Respect

As we confront the challenges of the 21st century, the UDHR remains a vital guide. Its principles call on all of us—governments, organizations, and individuals—to stand up for what is right and ensure that the promise of "freedom, justice, and peace in the world" becomes a reality for all.

Most importantly: Why Human Rights Matter Today

The Universal Declaration of Human Rights (UDHR) is not merely a relic of history; it is a living, breathing document that continues to resonate in the modern world. As humanity grapples with complex challenges, from climate change and economic inequality to political repression and technological surveillance, the UDHR serves as a guide and a call to action.

This chapter delves into contemporary issues threatening human rights and real-life stories of individuals and movements that have drawn strength from the UDHR to fight for justice and dignity.

Rising Authoritarianism and Suppression of Freedoms

In recent years, authoritarian regimes have surged worldwide, undermining democratic principles and human rights. Governments have restricted freedoms of speech, press, and assembly under the guise of maintaining order or combating misinformation.

Case Study: Journalists Under Siege

Maria Ressa, a journalist from the Philippines and Nobel Peace Prize laureate, has faced relentless persecution for her work exposing corruption and abuses of power under President Rodrigo Duterte's administration. Using Article 19 of the UDHR, which guarantees freedom of expression, Ressa has become a global symbol of the fight for press freedom.

In one of her interviews, Ressa said:
"If we don't have facts, we can't have truth. If we don't have truth, we can't have trust. Without these, democracy as we know it is dead."

Her case highlights the critical role of free press in holding governments accountable and the lengths to which authoritarian regimes will go to suppress dissent.

Crackdowns in Myanmar

In Myanmar, the military junta's violent suppression of pro-democracy protests following the 2021 coup serves as a chilling reminder of the fragility of human rights. The UDHR's Articles 21 (right to participate in government) and 20 (freedom of peaceful assembly) are routinely violated as thousands have been detained, tortured, or killed for resisting the regime.

Despite these atrocities, the people of Myanmar continue to fight for their rights, drawing international attention to their struggle. Activists like Wai Wai Nu, a former political prisoner turned global advocate, use the UDHR as a framework to demand action and solidarity.

Economic Inequality and the Right to Dignity
Economic inequality remains one of the greatest barriers to achieving universal human rights. The COVID-19 pandemic starkly illuminated these disparities, as vulnerable populations bore the brunt of its impacts.

Story: The Pandemic's Marginalized Victims
In India, millions of migrant workers were left stranded without food, shelter, or income during the nationwide lockdown in 2020. Forced to walk hundreds of miles to their villages, many succumbed to exhaustion, hunger, or illness.

The situation highlighted glaring violations of Article 25, which affirms the right to an adequate standard of living, and Article 23, which guarantees the right to work under just conditions. Civil society organizations stepped in where governments failed, providing aid and amplifying the voices of the marginalized.

One such story is that of Sneha, a 19-year-old domestic worker who lost her job during the pandemic. When interviewed, she said:

"I've always worked hard, but now there's no work, no food, and no way to survive. Is this what life is supposed to be?"

Her words echo the struggle of millions whose basic rights remain unfulfilled despite the promises of the UDHR.

Technology and Privacy: A New Battlefield
The digital age has created new opportunities for communication, education, and activism. However, it has also introduced significant threats to privacy, freedom, and security.

Mass Surveillance in China
In China, the government's use of mass surveillance technologies, such as facial recognition software and social credit systems, has raised alarms about violations of Article 12 of the UDHR, which protects against arbitrary interference with privacy. Uyghur Muslims in Xinjiang Province have faced the brunt of these measures, with surveillance technologies used to

track their movements and behavior. Many have been detained in so-called "re-education camps," where reports of forced labor and abuse abound.

Despite the risks, activists like Mihrigul Tursun, a Uyghur survivor, have spoken out. In a testimony to the U.S. Congress, she shared:

"My people are being watched every second of every day. They are punished for being who they are. The world cannot ignore this."

Online Harassment and Censorship
Social media platforms, while empowering, have also become tools for harassment and censorship. Women, minorities, and activists are often targeted with abuse, silencing their voices and violating their right to free expression. For instance, Ugandan activist Vanessa Nakate, an advocate for climate justice, has faced racial and gender-based online harassment. Despite this, she continues to use her platform to fight for environmental and human rights, emphasizing the interconnectedness of the two.

Environmental Justice: A Human Rights Issue
The climate crisis poses an existential threat to humanity, disproportionately affecting the most vulnerable populations. Articles 3 (right to life) and 25

(right to an adequate standard of living) are directly at stake as rising sea levels, extreme weather, and resource scarcity drive displacement and conflict.

Story: The Pacific Island Nations
In Kiribati, a small Pacific island nation, rising sea levels have submerged homes and forced entire communities to relocate. The country's president, Anote Tong, has called for global action, arguing that the climate crisis is a human rights crisis.

"Where will my people go?" he asked during a UN summit. "Our lands are disappearing. Our culture, our identity—everything we are—is at risk."

The UDHR provides a moral framework for addressing these issues, even as nations struggle to translate its principles into concrete action.

Movements for Justice and Equality
The UDHR's principles continue to inspire movements for justice and equality across the globe.

Black Lives Matter
The Black Lives Matter movement in the United States has used the UDHR as a foundation for demanding an end to police brutality and systemic racism. Protesters often cite Article 7, which

guarantees equality before the law, as they call for reforms to the justice system.

In a statement, Alicia Garza, one of the movement's founders, said:

"The UDHR reminds us that freedom and dignity are not just ideals—they are rights that belong to all of us. It's time we make that a reality."

Women's Rights in Afghanistan

Following the Taliban's return to power in Afghanistan, women and girls have faced severe restrictions on their rights to education, employment, and freedom of movement—violations of Articles 26 (right to education) and 23 (right to work).

Activists like Zarifa Ghafari, one of Afghanistan's first female mayors, have refused to stay silent. Ghafari, now in exile, continues to advocate for Afghan women, drawing on the UDHR to demand international intervention.

Conclusion: A Shared Responsibility

The stories and struggles explored in this chapter underscore the enduring importance of the UDHR. Its principles serve as both a shield and a sword—

The Power of Respect

a shield to protect the vulnerable and a sword to challenge injustice. In a world still grappling with inequality, conflict, and oppression, the UDHR reminds us of our shared humanity and collective responsibility. Its ideals may not yet be fully realized, but they remain a guiding light, calling us to build a future where freedom, justice, and dignity belong to everyone.

As Eleanor Roosevelt once said:
"Where, after all, do universal human rights begin? In small places, close to home. Unless these rights have meaning there, they have little meaning anywhere."

This is the challenge—and the promise—of human rights today.

The Power of Respect

Chapter 3: Humanity's Unyielding Spirit – My Personal Journey

Human rights are not merely abstract ideals—they are the essence of our shared humanity, shaped and reshaped by the lives of those who live, struggle, and advocate for them. My story is one of resilience, mistakes, and redemption, a testament to the complexities of life and the enduring power of compassion. By sharing the challenges I have faced and the lessons I have learned, I hope to inspire others to see that, no matter how daunting the road may seem, we all have the capacity to make a difference.

The Early Years: Seeds of Empathy
My childhood was a paradox of privilege and exposure to suffering. I was born into a family that gave me opportunities, yet from an early age, I was keenly aware of the inequalities that shaped our world. One memory stands out vividly. As a child, I often visited bustling marketplaces with my family. One afternoon, I saw a young boy, no older than ten, carrying a heavy sack of potatoes. His face was flushed

from the heat, and his clothes were tattered. He was working while other children played. I felt a pang of guilt as I sat comfortably in the car, holding a new toy. That moment planted a question in my heart: Why is life so unequal?

Years later, this memory would fuel my advocacy for children's rights. I realized that millions of children were robbed of their childhoods, forced to work under harsh conditions to support their families. That boy's face still reminds me why I fight for justice.

Hardships That Shaped Me

Life often tests us in ways we don't anticipate, pushing us to confront our vulnerabilities and redefine our understanding of strength. My journey has been shaped by trials that left lasting imprints on my identity, forcing me to adapt and grow in ways I never imagined.

One of the most haunting memories from my childhood occurred when I witnessed a school bus reversing and running over a little boy. I was only ten years old, and the trauma of that moment left a deep sadness within me. Unable to fully process the event, I began covering my hair and wearing black clothes, as if mirroring the grief and confusion I carried inside.

The Power of Respect

At such a young age, I didn't have the tools to make sense of the complexity of life or death, and my outward appearance became a reflection of my inner struggle.

As I grew older, I faced a different kind of challenge—one rooted in the opinions and judgments of others. People interfered in my life, casting doubts and assumptions about me, even though I had done nothing to deserve their criticism. Their envy and unkindness forced me to withdraw, to change my appearance and behavior in an effort to please them or shield myself from their negativity. I was a beautiful child and a beautiful woman, but my beauty seemed to provoke others, leading to cruelty I couldn't comprehend. At the time, I didn't understand how one human could deliberately hurt another, nor did I see that their opinions were more about their own insecurities than about me.

Over time, I found solace in learning about human rights and the importance of setting boundaries. This knowledge transformed my perspective, helping me reclaim my confidence and sense of self. I realized that my worth isn't determined by the opinions of others. Their judgments are merely reflections of how they see themselves, projected outward. By understanding this, I learned to separate their negativity from my

The Power of Respect

identity, freeing myself from the need to conform to their expectations. Today, I see strength not as the absence of vulnerability but as the ability to rise above it. I respect myself and demand the same from others, setting boundaries that protect my peace and allow me to thrive. The trials I faced taught me that growth often comes through pain, and true empowerment begins with self-respect and understanding.

My journey has shown me that life's challenges, though painful, can be profound teachers. They teach us resilience, self-awareness, and the importance of advocating for our own well-being. Through these lessons, I've come to see my vulnerabilities not as weaknesses but as stepping stones to a more authentic and empowered version of myself.

The Burden of Public Scrutiny

Years ago, my personal life became a matter of public discussion, and not always in a flattering light. Decisions I made were dissected, misinterpreted, and judged by people who knew little of my circumstances. Headlines were harsh, and whispers followed me everywhere I went.

I vividly remember reading an article about myself, filled with inaccuracies and cruel assumptions. It felt like a betrayal—not just by the media, but by society's tendency to reduce people to their mistakes.

In those moments, I questioned everything. How could I continue advocating for others when I couldn't even shield myself from criticism? But over time, I realized that these experiences had given me a deeper empathy for those whose lives are misunderstood or marginalized. If I could survive public scrutiny, I could channel that resilience into fighting for those without a voice.

The Loss That Changed Everything
One of the hardest periods of my life came with the loss of someone I loved deeply. Grief is a heavy, unrelenting shadow, and for a time, it consumed me. I withdrew from the world, feeling like I had nothing left to give.

It was during this time that I discovered the healing power of service. Volunteering at a shelter for displaced families gave me a renewed sense of purpose. I saw mothers who had lost everything still smiling for their children. I saw children finding joy in the smallest things. Their resilience reminded me that even in our darkest moments, there is light to be found.

The Power of Respect

Advocacy and the Causes Close to My Heart

The challenges I faced taught me the importance of using my voice and privilege to uplift others. Over the years, I have been involved in various initiatives aimed at promoting human rights and dignity.

Empowering Women and Girls: Building a Future of Equality

One of the most significant focuses of my work has been empowering women and girls, especially those in underserved communities. I believe that when women thrive, entire communities benefit. This belief has driven initiatives aimed at education, economic empowerment, and creating safe spaces for women to grow.

Transforming Lives Through Education

The story of Aicha, the young girl from a rural village, is just one example of how access to education can change a life. Through scholarships and partnerships with local organizations, we've enabled hundreds of girls to pursue their studies.

One unforgettable experience was visiting a village where girls were traditionally barred from attending school. I met Aisha, a 12-year-old who was forced to drop out of school to care for her siblings while her parents worked. Aisha's eyes lit up as she told me about her dream of becoming a doctor—a dream she thought was impossible. By working with her family and community leaders, we were able to enroll Aisha in a boarding school that provided not only education but also the support she needed to thrive. Today, Aisha is studying biology and plans to return to her village as a physician.

Economic Empowerment Programs
While education is a cornerstone, economic independence is equally vital for women's empowerment. Many of the women I've worked with faced barriers to employment due to cultural norms, lack of resources, or inadequate training.

In 2020, while activating for conservatives we launched an initiative to provide micro loans and skill-building workshops to women in rural communities. I recall meeting Anna, a widowed mother of three, who had struggled to make ends meet after losing her husband. With a small loan and training in tailoring, Anna started a clothing business. Her resilience turned her into a community leader, inspiring other women to seek opportunities for independence. Anna once told me, "I thought my life was over, but now I see that I have the power to shape my future. Thank you for believing in me."

The Power of Respect

Advocating Against Gender-Based Violence
Gender-based violence remains one of the most pervasive violations of women's rights worldwide. My advocacy has focused on both prevention and support for survivors. Through partnerships with shelters and legal aid organizations, we've provided resources for women to escape abusive situations and rebuild their lives.

One heart-wrenching story involves Leyla, a young woman who fled her home after enduring years of abuse. When we met, she was hesitant to trust anyone. Through counseling and mentorship, Leyla found her voice again. She now works with us as an advocate, helping other women break free from cycles of violence.

Humanitarian Aid: A Lifeline for the Vulnerable
My work with displaced families and refugees has been one of the most challenging yet rewarding aspects of my journey. Witnessing their resilience has deepened my commitment to ensuring that no one is forgotten.

The Syrian Refugee Crisis
One of the most profound experiences of my life was visiting a refugee camp near the Syrian border. The camp was overcrowded, with families living in

makeshift shelters that barely protected them from the elements. Despite the dire conditions, the spirit of the people was unbreakable.

I met Rami, a 9-year-old boy who had lost both parents in the conflict. He clung to his younger sister, acting as her protector and caretaker. Their story moved me to tears. Through our initiative, we provided resources for education and psychological support, ensuring that Rami and his sister could begin to heal.

Feeding the Hungry
Food insecurity is another critical issue we address. During one of our relief missions, I joined a team distributing meals to displaced families in Yemen. The lines stretched endlessly, with mothers cradling malnourished babies and children holding empty bowls. In the chaos of the distribution, a young girl named Hana approached me with a shy smile. She handed me a drawing of a sunflower she had made on a scrap of paper. When I asked her why she chose a sunflower, she said, "Because it always finds the sun, even in the darkness." That moment encapsulated the resilience I've witnessed in so many of the people we serve. It drives me to continue fighting for their right to a dignified life.

The Power of Respect

Mental Health Advocacy: Breaking the Silence
Mental health is an integral yet often overlooked component of human rights, and organizations which I'm a patron & ambassador of peace for as the Universal Peace Federation (UPF) and United Nations Women are playing pivotal roles in addressing these challenges, particularly in marginalized communities. Both organizations emphasize the importance of reducing stigma, fostering awareness, and building supportive environments for mental health.

The Universal Peace Federation (UPF), a global network committed to fostering peace and understanding, actively incorporates mental health advocacy in its programs. For instance, its UK chapter has hosted events focusing on women's safety and empowerment, which often address the mental health impacts of issues like domestic violence. UPF collaborates with diverse stakeholders, including parliamentarians and NGOs, to create actionable solutions for vulnerable groups, ensuring that mental health concerns are integrated into discussions about human rights and peace building.

Similarly, United Nations Women focuses on creating inclusive systems to tackle gender-based challenges, including mental health. By promoting gender equality, supporting survivors of violence, and encouraging leadership roles for women, the organization ensures that mental well-being is part of the broader human rights framework. Their programs work to dismantle stigma, provide resources for recovery, and advocate for systemic change to protect the psychological and emotional health of women and girls globally.

These initiatives collectively highlight the importance of mental health as a human right. By educating communities, empowering individuals, and creating safe spaces for dialogue, organizations like UPF and (UN) United Nations (WHO) world, health, organization, are ensuring that mental health is not sidelined but is treated as a critical element of achieving global peace and equality. Through their work, they remind us that mental well-being is fundamental to human dignity and progress.

Creating Safe Spaces
One of our flagship initiatives is a mental health support program for young people dealing with trauma. During a workshop I attended, I heard the story of Ahmed, a teenager who had lost his father to violence and was struggling with anger and grief. Through group therapy sessions, Ahmed found a way to process his emotions and channel them into art.

The Power of Respect

His paintings, now displayed in local galleries, tell a story of pain and healing that resonates deeply.

Public Awareness Campaigns

I've also worked to destigmatize mental health challenges through public awareness campaigns. Partnering with local leaders and media outlets, we've reached thousands of people with messages of hope and support.

One of our most impactful campaigns featured survivors of trauma sharing their journeys to recovery. Their courage has inspired others to seek help, breaking the cycle of silence and shame.

Cultural Preservation: A Fight for Identity

In my travels, I've encountered communities whose cultures and traditions are at risk of disappearing due to conflict, displacement, or globalization. Preserving these cultural identities is essential for maintaining the dignity and history of these groups.

The Bedouin Weavers of the Middle East

During a visit to a remote Bedouin community, I met a group of women who wove intricate patterns into rugs and garments. Their craft was not just a livelihood—it was a link to their heritage. However, with younger generations moving to cities, these traditions were fading.

Through funding and training programs, we helped establish a cooperative that allowed the women to sell their crafts internationally. The cooperative has not only revived the tradition but also provided financial independence for the women involved.

One of the weavers, Yasmina, told me, "Every thread I weave carries the story of my ancestors. Thank you for helping us keep our stories alive."

Language Preservation
In collaboration with linguists and cultural organizations, we've worked to document endangered languages spoken by displaced communities. This effort has included creating educational materials and recording oral histories, ensuring that these languages are not lost to time.

The Broader Impact: From Individuals to Systems
While individual stories are at the heart of my work, the broader impact lies in systemic change. Advocacy at the policy level has been crucial in amplifying the voices of those we serve.

The Power of Respect

Influencing Policy
Through partnerships with international organizations, I've had the opportunity to speak at global forums, advocating for policies that prioritize human rights. Whether addressing the UN on refugee rights or participating in panels on gender equality, my goal is to ensure that these issues remain at the forefront of international discourse.

Building Alliances
Collaboration has been key to expanding the reach of our initiatives. By partnering with NGOs, local governments, and grassroots organizations, we've been able to scale our efforts and create sustainable change.

A Legacy of Compassion
Looking back on my journey, I am filled with gratitude for the opportunity to serve. The challenges I have faced and the people I have met have shaped me in ways I never imagined.

If there is one message I hope to leave behind, it is this: every act of kindness, no matter how small, has the power to ripple outward and create change. Together, we can build a world where dignity, justice, and hope are not just ideals but realities for all.

Chapter 4: Strategies Behind the Initiatives – Duchess Nivin ElGamal's Blueprint for Change

Transforming lives and advocating for human rights requires more than passion—it demands careful planning, strategic execution, and an unwavering commitment to sustainability. Over the years, I've developed a multi-faceted approach to ensure my initiatives address immediate needs while creating lasting impact. This chapter explores the strategies behind my work, highlighting how each step is designed to maximize effectiveness and empower communities.

1. Listening to Communities: Needs-Based Solutions

One of the first lessons I learned in advocacy was that assumptions can undermine good intentions. No matter how well-meaning an initiative may seem, its success depends on addressing the real needs of the community.

The Power of Respect

Building Trust Through Dialogue
Before launching any project, I ensure that we spend significant time engaging with the community. This involves hosting focus groups, conducting surveys, and holding one-on-one conversations to understand their unique challenges and aspirations. For example, during a visit to a rural village where education rates were low, I initially thought the lack of schools was the main barrier. However, after speaking with families, I discovered that many parents were reluctant to send their daughters to school because of safety concerns during their commute. This insight led us to prioritize building schools within the village and providing safe transportation for students.

Empowering Local Leaders
Another key strategy is working with local leaders who understand the cultural and social dynamics of their communities. These leaders act as bridges, helping us tailor our initiatives to align with local customs and values while ensuring that the community feels ownership over the project.

2. Focusing on Education as a Catalyst for Change

Education is at the heart of many of my initiatives because it is a powerful tool for breaking the cycle of poverty and inequality.

To maximize the impact of educational programs, I've adopted a three-pronged approach: access, quality, and relevance.

Improving Access

Many of the communities I work with face significant barriers to education, including poverty, distance, and cultural norms. To address these challenges, I've prioritized:

- Building Infrastructure: Constructing schools in underserved areas.
- Providing Scholarships: Offering financial support to families who cannot afford tuition or school supplies.
- Leveraging Technology: Introducing mobile classrooms and online learning platforms in remote areas.

One particularly successful initiative involved establishing solar-powered classrooms in a remote village with no access to electricity. This allowed students to attend evening classes, giving them a chance to learn without disrupting their daily chores.

Ensuring Quality

Access to education is meaningless without quality. To this end, we invest in teacher training, curriculum development, and providing modern teaching materials. By partnering with educational organizations, we've introduced programs that focus on critical thinking, creativity, and problem-solving rather than rote memorization.

Promoting Relevance

Education should prepare individuals for the realities of their world. In addition to academic subjects, we incorporate vocational training and life skills into the curriculum. For example, in agricultural communities, we've introduced courses on sustainable farming techniques, empowering students to apply their learning directly to their environment.

3. Economic Empowerment: Building Sustainable Livelihoods

Economic empowerment is a cornerstone of my work because financial independence gives individuals the freedom to make choices and assert their rights.

Microfinance and Entrepreneurship

One of the most impactful strategies has been offering microloans to individuals, particularly women, to start small businesses. These loans are often paired with workshops on financial literacy, marketing, and business management.

For instance, in a project targeting urban slums, we provided loans to women who wanted to start tailoring businesses. Over time, many of these women not only repaid their loans but also hired others, creating a ripple effect of economic growth within their communities.

Skill Development Programs
Recognizing that many individuals lack the skills needed to access better opportunities, we've launched vocational training programs in areas such as:
- Tailoring and Handicrafts
- Computer Skills
- Agriculture and Animal Husbandry

By tailoring these programs to the local job market, we ensure that participants are equipped with skills that translate directly into income-generating opportunities.

4. Advocacy and Awareness: Amplifying Voices
While direct interventions are vital, systemic change requires raising awareness and influencing public opinion. Advocacy and awareness campaigns are

central to my work, ensuring that the issues we address gain the attention they deserve.

Media Campaigns

Partnering with media outlets has allowed us to amplify the stories of the people we serve, humanizing their struggles and inspiring action. Whether through documentaries, social media posts, or public service announcements, we use storytelling to create empathy and drive change. One memorable campaign featured a series of short films documenting the lives of refugee families. These films, shared widely on social media, helped raise funds for our programs while fostering greater understanding of the refugee crisis.

Engaging Influencers and Ambassadors

Another effective strategy has been enlisting the support of influential figures to champion our causes. By leveraging their platforms, we've reached wider audiences and sparked conversations around issues like gender equality and mental health.

5. Collaboration and Partnerships: Strength in Numbers

No organization can solve systemic issues alone. Collaboration with like-minded organizations, governments, and individuals is essential for scaling impact and ensuring sustainability.

Forming Alliances
Through partnerships with NGOs, we've been able to pool resources and expertise to tackle complex challenges. For example, our collaboration with a healthcare nonprofit allowed us to bring mobile clinics to remote areas, providing essential medical care to thousands.

Engaging Governments
Working with local and national governments has been instrumental in creating long-term change. By advocating for policy reforms and supporting government-led initiatives, we've ensured that our programs align with broader development goals.

6. Addressing Mental Health: A Holistic Approach

Mental health is integral to overall well-being, yet it is often neglected in humanitarian work. To address this gap, we've implemented a holistic approach that combines counseling, community support, and public education.

Community-Based Counseling

Recognizing that professional mental health services are often inaccessible in underserved areas, we've trained community members to provide basic counseling. These counselors act as the first line of support, offering guidance and connecting individuals to professional help when needed.

Creating Safe Spaces

Through group therapy sessions and peer support networks, we've created environments where individuals can share their struggles without fear of judgment. These spaces have been particularly effective for survivors of trauma, including refugees and victims of gender-based violence.

7. Monitoring and Evaluation: Ensuring Accountability

To ensure that our initiatives are effective and sustainable, we place a strong emphasis on monitoring and evaluation.

Setting Clear Goals

Every project begins with clearly defined objectives and measurable outcomes. Whether it's increasing school enrollment rates or improving access to clean water, we establish benchmarks to track progress.

Collecting Data
We use a combination of surveys, interviews, and on-the-ground observations to gather data on the impact of our initiatives. This allows us to identify areas for improvement and make data-driven decisions.

Incorporating Feedback
Feedback from the communities we serve is invaluable. Regular check-ins ensure that our programs remain relevant and responsive to their needs.

8. Sustainability: Leaving a Lasting Impact
True success lies in creating programs that outlast our direct involvement. To achieve this, we focus on building local capacity and fostering self-reliance.

Training Community Leaders
By equipping community members with the skills and knowledge to manage programs independently, we ensure that the impact of our work continues long after we leave.

Promoting Ownership
Encouraging communities to take ownership of projects instills a sense of pride and responsibility. For example, in a water sanitation project, local

committees were formed to oversee maintenance and operations, ensuring the project's longevity.

A Vision for the Future
As I reflect on the strategies that have guided my work, I am reminded of the incredible potential within every individual and community. The road ahead is long, but I remain committed to creating a world where every person has the opportunity to live with dignity and hope.

By combining compassion with strategy, we can turn aspirations into actions and dreams into realities. Together, we can continue building a legacy of empowerment, resilience, and change.

Chapter 5: Lessons Learned from Implementing Change

As much as advocacy and humanitarian work are about helping others, they are also deeply transformative for the individuals leading these efforts. Over the years, I've gained invaluable insights from the challenges and triumphs of implementing initiatives. These lessons have not only shaped my approach to advocacy but have also taught me profound truths about leadership, collaboration, and the resilience of the human spirit.

This chapter shares the key lessons I've learned from my work, offering guidance for those who aspire to create meaningful change.

1. **The Importance of Listening**
One of the first and most critical lessons I learned was that listening is the foundation of effective advocacy. Even with the best intentions, it's easy to fall into the trap of assuming we know what's best for others.

The Power of Respect

Lesson in Action: A Community's True Needs
During an early project aimed at increasing school attendance in a rural village, we focused on providing textbooks and supplies, assuming these were the primary barriers to education. However, after speaking with families, we discovered that the real issue was a lack of access to clean water. Children spent hours fetching water each day, leaving little time for school.

This experience taught me that understanding a community's true needs requires active listening and an openness to adapt. Once we prioritized building a well, school attendance rose significantly.

Takeaway: Change begins with understanding. Listen first, act second.

2. **Collaboration Over Control**
Another vital lesson has been the power of collaboration. No matter how capable or passionate you are, achieving systemic change is impossible without partnerships.

Lesson in Action: Partnering with Local Leaders
In one initiative to support women entrepreneurs, I initially struggled to gain traction. Many women were

hesitant to participate, fearing backlash from their communities. By partnering with local religious and community leaders, we gained their trust and support, which ultimately encouraged the women to join the program.

This collaboration not only enhanced the program's success but also ensured it was culturally sensitive and sustainable.

Takeaway: Collaboration fosters trust, amplifies impact, and creates long-term change.

3. Flexibility is Key

Advocacy work rarely goes according to plan. External factors like political instability, natural disasters, or cultural resistance can disrupt even the most well-thought-out initiatives. Flexibility is essential to navigate these challenges.

Lesson in Action: Adapting During the Pandemic

The COVID-19 pandemic disrupted many of our projects, particularly those involving in-person workshops and community gatherings. Rather than putting everything on hold, we pivoted to online platforms and mobile outreach programs. For instance, we launched a telehealth initiative to provide mental health support, which ended up reaching far more people than we initially anticipated.

Takeaway: Being adaptable allows you to turn challenges into opportunities.

4. Empowerment is More Sustainable than Charity

While immediate aid is essential in times of crisis, long-term change comes from empowering individuals and communities to take charge of their futures.

Lesson in Action: Transitioning from Aid to Ownership

In one refugee camp, our initial focus was on providing food and shelter. Over time, we shifted to programs that taught residents skills like farming and sewing, enabling them to generate income and support their families. Today, many of these individuals have become leaders within their communities, helping others in similar situations.

Takeaway: Empowerment builds resilience, dignity, and lasting impact.

5. Addressing Root Causes, Not Just Symptoms

It's tempting to focus on visible problems, but true advocacy requires digging deeper to address the underlying causes of those issues.

Lesson in Action: Tackling Gender Inequality

In one community, we noticed that women were excluded from decision-making processes, which hindered their access to education and employment. Rather than simply providing resources, we launched a series of workshops for men and women, emphasizing the benefits of gender equality. Over time, attitudes shifted, and women began to play more active roles in their communities.

Takeaway: Addressing root causes leads to systemic change rather than temporary fixes.

6. Balancing Compassion with Practicality

Advocacy work often involves heartbreaking stories and overwhelming challenges. While compassion is essential, maintaining a practical mindset is equally important to create measurable impact.

Lesson in Action: Setting Realistic Goals

Early in my career, I often overpromised in my eagerness to help, leading to burnout and frustration when goals weren't met. I learned to focus on what could realistically be achieved with the available resources, ensuring that every promise made was a promise kept.

Takeaway: Compassion must be tempered with realism to achieve sustainable progress.

7. The Power of Storytelling
Human rights advocacy is about more than programs and policies—it's about people. Stories have the power to inspire action, build empathy, and mobilize support.

Lesson in Action: Hana's Sunflower
The story of Hana, the young refugee who gave me a drawing of a sunflower, became a central part of our campaign to raise awareness about food insecurity. Her simple yet powerful message—"sunflowers find the sun even in darkness"—resonated with donors and policymakers alike, resulting in a significant increase in funding for our programs.

Takeaway: Never underestimate the power of a personal story to inspire change.

8. Self-Care is Non-Negotiable

Advocacy work can be emotionally and physically exhausting. Early in my journey, I neglected my own well-being, leading to burnout that affected both my personal and professional life.

Lesson in Action: Prioritizing Mental Health

After experiencing burnout, I made self-care a priority. This included seeking therapy, delegating responsibilities, and setting boundaries. By taking care of myself, I became a more effective leader and advocate.

Takeaway: You cannot pour from an empty cup. Taking care of yourself is essential to taking care of others.

9. The Value of Patience

Change is often slow and incremental. One of the hardest lessons I've learned is the importance of patience, especially when progress feels frustratingly slow.

Lesson in Action: Progress in Gender Equality

In one rural community, it took years of advocacy, dialogue, and small wins to shift deeply ingrained gender norms. While the change was gradual, seeing women step into leadership roles and girls attend school for the first time was a powerful reminder that patience pays off.

Takeaway: Change takes time, but persistence and patience yield results.

10. The Ripple Effect of Small Actions

It's easy to feel overwhelmed by the magnitude of global issues, but even small actions can create ripples of change that extend far beyond what we imagine.

Lesson in Action: A Single Sewing Machine

In one project, we provided a sewing machine to a woman named Noor, who used it to start a small tailoring business. Over time, Noor's business grew, and she began teaching other women her trade. Today, her sewing cooperative employs over 20 women, transforming not just her life but her entire community.

Takeaway: Never underestimate the impact of small, meaningful actions.

Conclusion: Lessons for a Lifetime

The journey of advocacy has been as much about personal growth as it has been about creating change. Each lesson learned has strengthened my resolve and deepened my understanding of what it means to serve others.

If there's one overarching truth I've discovered, it's this: humanity is resilient, compassionate, and capable of extraordinary transformation when given the tools and opportunities to thrive.

To those who aspire to make a difference, I offer this advice: listen, collaborate, adapt, and never lose sight of the people you serve. Together, we can continue building a world where dignity, justice, and hope are realities for all.

Chapter 6: The Power of Respect – A Cornerstone of Peace

Respect is not an instinct; it is a skill, a value, and a practice that must be nurtured and taught. It forms the foundation of personal relationships, community harmony, and global peace. In a world where division and conflict often take center stage, teaching respect and fostering it across generations has never been more urgent.

This chapter delves deeper into the necessity of teaching respect, its role in broader peacebuilding efforts, and how it transforms lives and societies. Through specific anecdotes and broader reflections, we explore how respect bridges divides and paves the way for coexistence.

Teaching Respect: The Foundation of Character
Respect is learned behavior. While some may develop it through experience, others require deliberate guidance to understand its value. Teaching respect—both at home and in schools—is the first step toward building a more empathetic and peaceful society.

The Power of Respect

Anecdote: The Classroom of Understanding
In a conflict-affected region, I once visited a school where tensions between students of different ethnic backgrounds were palpable. The principal shared how arguments often escalated into fights, creating a toxic environment. We introduced a *"Respect Curriculum"* that incorporated storytelling, role-playing, and collaborative activities. One memorable exercise involved students sharing personal objects that held sentimental value and explaining why they were important.

A boy named Karim brought an old photograph of his grandmother, while a girl named Amina shared a bracelet her mother had made. As they listened to each other, their expressions softened. By the end of the session, they realized they had more in common than they thought—both cherished their families and longed for stability.

Over time, the students began to respect one another's differences, and the school transformed into a more inclusive space.

Lesson: Teaching respect begins with creating opportunities for empathy and understanding. When children learn to value others' perspectives, they carry those lessons into adulthood.

The Power of Respect

Respect in Families: The Seeds of Peace
The family is where respect is first cultivated—or neglected. Children learn by observing how their elders treat one another and the world around them.

Anecdote: The Father's Apology
During a community workshop on family dynamics, a father stood up and shared his story. He admitted that he had been dismissive of his children's opinions, often silencing them with phrases like, *"You don't know what you're talking about."

One day, his youngest son refused to speak at all, even when asked a question. It was a wake-up call for the father, who realized he had inadvertently taught his children that their voices didn't matter.

He apologized to his family and began making a conscious effort to listen. Over time, his children became more confident and open, and the household dynamic shifted toward mutual respect.

Lesson: Families are the first schools of respect. When parents model respect in their words and actions, they instill values that last a lifetime.

The Power of Respect

Respect in Broader Peacebuilding Efforts
At the global level, respect is essential for resolving conflicts, rebuilding trust, and fostering cooperation among nations. It serves as both a moral principle and a practical tool for diplomacy and reconciliation.

Anecdote: The Mediator's Respect
In a post-conflict zone where two ethnic groups had been at war, international mediators struggled to bring both sides to the negotiation table. The breakthrough came when one mediator, a seasoned diplomat, took a radically different approach: he began by visiting each community, not to negotiate but to listen.

He spent hours sitting with elders, asking about their histories, traditions, and grievances. He respected their stories without judgment, which earned him their trust. When negotiations resumed, the mediator opened the session by recounting what he had learned about each group's heritage and values.

This act of respect disarmed both sides, showing them that their identities were recognized and valued. The negotiations progressed, leading to agreements that respected the autonomy and dignity of both communities.

The Power of Respect

Lesson: In peacebuilding, respect is not a sign of weakness but a demonstration of strength and commitment. It creates the conditions for genuine dialogue and compromise.

Respecting Nature: A Path to Peace
Respect is not limited to human relationships; it extends to the natural world. Environmental degradation often exacerbates conflicts, particularly in regions where resources like water and arable land are scarce. Teaching respect for nature is essential for both ecological sustainability and global peace.

Anecdote: The River Guardians
In a drought-stricken region, tensions flared between neighboring communities competing for access to a dwindling river. Violence seemed inevitable until a joint initiative brought the two groups together to address the issue collaboratively.

Elders from both communities agreed to establish a "River Guardians" program, where representatives from each group worked together to monitor water usage and implement conservation practices.

During a meeting, one elder said, "The river doesn't belong to any one of us—it belongs to all of us. Respecting it means respecting each other."

The Power of Respect

The program not only reduced tensions but also restored the river's flow, benefiting both communities.

Lesson: Respect for the environment is deeply intertwined with respect for each other. Sustainable peace requires honoring our shared responsibility to protect the planet.

The Role of Cultural Respect in Bridging Divides
Cultural differences are often seen as barriers, but when approached with respect, they become opportunities for enrichment and connection.

Anecdote: The Shared Meal
In a multicultural city, a community center organized a "Cultural Exchange Dinner" to address rising tensions between immigrant and local populations. Families from different backgrounds were invited to share traditional dishes and the stories behind them.

One local family brought a pot of stew, a recipe passed down through generations, while an immigrant family brought a dish made with spices unfamiliar to many. As they exchanged recipes and sampled each other's food, conversations blossomed.

The Power of Respect

A local woman remarked, "I used to think they were so different from us, but their family values and traditions remind me of my own."

The event became an annual tradition, fostering a sense of unity in diversity.

Lesson: Respect for cultural differences builds bridges of understanding. Celebrating diversity enriches communities and strengthens social cohesion.

Teaching Respect in Schools: A Long-Term Investment

Schools play a crucial role in shaping the values of future generations. Incorporating respect into the curriculum ensures that children grow up with the tools to navigate a diverse and interconnected world.

Anecdote: The Circle of Respect

In a pilot program for teaching respect in schools, we introduced an activity called the "Circle of Respect." Each student was given a turn to share something they appreciated about a classmate.

At first, some students hesitated, unsure of what to say. But as the activity progressed, the room filled with affirmations: "I like how you always help others," or "You're really good at making people laugh."

One shy student, who rarely spoke in class, received so much encouragement that he began participating more actively in lessons. The activity not only boosted individual confidence but also strengthened the sense of community within the classroom.

Lesson: Teaching respect in schools creates a ripple effect, fostering empathy, confidence, and collaboration among students.

Conclusion: Respect as the Bedrock of Peace

Respect is not merely an abstract ideal—it is a practice that shapes our interactions and determines the quality of our relationships, communities, and societies. It is the antidote to division, the bridge across conflict, and the foundation of peace.

Teaching respect requires effort, intention, and patience. It begins with small acts: listening to a child, acknowledging a neighbor's perspective, or honoring a cultural tradition. These acts, repeated consistently, create ripples that extend far beyond their immediate impact.

The Power of Respect

In a world that often feels fractured, respect reminds us of our shared humanity. By teaching and practicing it in every sphere of life, we can create a future where peace is not just an aspiration but a reality.

To those who read this, I urge you to carry the torch of respect in your daily lives. Teach it to your children, embody it in your relationships, and demand it in your communities. Together, we can build a world where respect lays the foundation for enduring peace.

The Power of Respect

Chapter 7: Respect as the Pillar of Human Rights – A Global Perspective

Respect is the cornerstone of human rights. It underpins every article of the Universal Declaration of Human Rights (UDHR), from the right to dignity and equality to the freedoms of thought, speech, and belief. It is the foundation for peace within ourselves, our communities, and the world at large. In this final chapter, I delve into the role of respect in addressing global conflicts, its place in education as a tool for transformation, and the enduring importance of the United Nations and the UDHR. By weaving in personal anecdotes, reflections from my Instagram posts, and a message for future generations, this chapter serves as a call to action: to practice and teach respect in all its forms, for the betterment of humanity.

Respect in Global Conflicts: A Path to Reconciliation

Conflicts often arise from a lack of respect—whether it's for cultural differences, territorial boundaries, or

The Power of Respect

human dignity. In global peacebuilding efforts, respect is not just a value but a tool for healing and reconciliation.

Anecdote: The Conflict in Sudan

During a visit to Sudan, I met with community leaders from two tribes that had been locked in violent disputes over land. The violence had displaced thousands and left scars of mistrust. Efforts to mediate had failed, as both sides viewed the other with hostility.

When I spoke to the elders, I focused not on their grievances but on their shared humanity. I asked each elder to describe a time when their tribe had shown kindness to the other. At first, the room was silent. Then, an elder from one tribe recounted how the other had once shared water during a drought.

This simple act of acknowledgment shifted the tone of the meeting. By focusing on mutual respect and shared history, we paved the way for further dialogue. Eventually, the tribes agreed to a peace accord that included resource-sharing agreements and cultural exchange programs.

The Power of Respect

Lesson: Respect is the first step in breaking cycles of conflict. It reminds people of their shared humanity and opens the door to healing.

Education as a Tool for Respect

Teaching respect in educational settings is one of the most powerful ways to create lasting change. When young people learn to respect themselves, their peers, and their communities, they become ambassadors for peace and equality.

Anecdote: The Girls of Kabul

In Afghanistan, where girls' education has often been restricted, I worked with local organizations to establish safe learning spaces. One day, I visited a school in Kabul and asked the students what they wanted to learn.

One girl, Fatima, stood up and said, *"I want to learn how to change the world, but first I need to learn how to respect it."* Her words struck me deeply.

We designed a curriculum that combined academic subjects with lessons on respect—respect for oneself, for others, and for cultural diversity. Over time, the girls not only excelled academically but also became advocates for their right to education, inspiring others in their community to join them.

The Power of Respect

Lesson: Education is not just about knowledge; it is about values. Teaching respect empowers young people to become agents of change.

The Role of the United Nations and the UDHR
The creation of the United Nations in 1945 and the adoption of the Universal Declaration of Human Rights in 1948 were monumental steps in humanity's journey toward peace and equality. These institutions remind us of the power of unity and the importance of a shared commitment to human dignity.

The History of the UN and the UDHR
The United Nations was established in the aftermath of World War II, when the world recognized the need for a global body to prevent future conflicts and promote cooperation. The UDHR, drafted shortly after, became the moral foundation of the UN's mission.

Eleanor Roosevelt, chair of the UDHR drafting committee, called it "the international Magna Carta of all mankind." Its 30 articles encompass civil, political, economic, social, and cultural rights, affirming that every human being is born free and equal in dignity and rights.

The Power of Respect

The Importance of the UN Today
The United Nations remains vital in addressing global challenges, from climate change and humanitarian crises to peacekeeping and human rights advocacy. It serves as a platform where nations can come together to resolve disputes, provide aid, and uphold the principles of the UDHR.

In one of my Instagram posts, I reflected on the enduring relevance of the UN:
"The United Nations is not just an institution; it is a promise—a promise to protect the vulnerable, to uphold justice, and to work toward a world where every individual's dignity is respected."

Respect is the invisible thread that holds humanity together. It is woven into the fabric of the Universal Declaration of Human Rights (UDHR), reminding us that dignity, equality, and justice are not privileges but birthrights. As we look toward a future shaped by the choices we make today, respect becomes our most powerful tool for achieving lasting peace.

This final chapter builds on my reflections shared on Instagram, emphasizing the role of respect in human rights advocacy, global peacebuilding, and education. Through expanded themes and a personal call to action, I invite you to join me in building a world where peace begins with respect.

Reflections from My Instagram: Respect & Peace

As a passionate advocate for human rights, I've used my Instagram platform, [@Duchess_NivinELGAMAL_Official] (https://www.instagram.com/Duchess_NivinELGAMAL_Official), to share thoughts, stories, and calls to action. Here are expanded reflections from my posts, highlighting the central role of respect in achieving peace:

1. Respect as a Foundation for Equality

"Every act of oppression begins with a lack of respect for another's dignity. Every act of justice begins with restoring that respect." This post was inspired by my experiences working with marginalized communities. I have seen how discrimination and inequality stem from a failure to respect differences. But I have also witnessed the transformative power of respect in restoring equality and hope.

2. Teaching Respect to the Next Generation

"Children are the architects of tomorrow's peace. Let's teach them that respect is not optional—it is essential."

The Power of Respect

This reflection came after visiting a school where students from diverse backgrounds learned about cultural respect through art and storytelling. Watching them celebrate each other's heritage reminded me that peace is a learned behavior, and education is its strongest ally.

3. Respect for the Planet

"We cannot claim to respect each other if we destroy the home we share. Environmental respect is human respect."

I shared this after participating in an environmental cleanup campaign alongside refugees who understood that protecting the planet is part of protecting our collective future. Respect for nature is inseparable from respect for humanity.

4. Respect in Everyday Actions

"Peace doesn't begin in conference rooms or parliaments. It begins in how we treat each other every day—with kindness, patience, and respect."

This post reflected on a simple moment: offering a warm smile to a stranger. It reminded me that peace is not just a lofty ideal—it's a daily practice.

Specific Themes to Complete the Path to Peace

Achieving peace requires a holistic approach that integrates respect into every aspect of life. Below are additional themes that emphasize how respect can lead to lasting peace:

1. Respecting Vulnerability: The Strength in Acknowledging Weakness

Peace does not demand perfection. It requires the courage to acknowledge vulnerability and the humility to address it.

Anecdote: Refugee Resilience

In a refugee camp I visited, a young woman named Samar shared her story. She had lost her home, her family, and her sense of safety. Yet, what struck me was her strength in admitting her fear and her determination to rebuild her life.

By respecting her vulnerability and offering support without pity, we empowered Samar to lead a counseling group for other women in the camp. She transformed her pain into a source of strength for others.

The Power of Respect

Lesson: Respecting vulnerability creates a safe space for healing and growth. It is a critical step toward building peace.

2. Respect in Leadership: Leading with Integrity

True leadership is grounded in respect—for oneself, for others, and for the principles that guide humanity.

Anecdote: The Young Activist

During a youth leadership summit, I met a young activist named Jamal, who was advocating for better education in his community. His passion was undeniable, but what made him a true leader was his ability to listen.

Jamal respected the ideas of his peers, even when they challenged his own. By fostering an environment of mutual respect, he united his group and achieved his goal of securing scholarships for underprivileged students.

Lesson: Respectful leadership inspires trust and collaboration, making it a powerful force for peace.

The Power of Respect

3. Respect Across Borders: Global Solidarity

Respect knows no boundaries. In a world divided by politics, religion, and culture, respect for diversity is the key to global solidarity.

Anecdote: The International Workshop

At an international workshop on women's rights, participants from over 20 countries shared their struggles and successes. Despite their different backgrounds, they found common ground in their shared vision for gender equality.

One participant from India said, "I thought my challenges were unique, but hearing your stories makes me realize we are fighting the same battle."

This sense of global solidarity, rooted in mutual respect, amplified their collective voice and strengthened their resolve.

Lesson: Respect for diversity fosters unity, enabling us to address global challenges together.

4. Respect for Future Generations: Environmental Sustainability

Respect for the planet is a moral obligation to future generations. Peace is impossible in a world plagued by resource scarcity, climate-induced displacement, and environmental degradation.

Anecdote: Planting Hope
In a reforestation project, I worked alongside children and elders to plant trees in a deforested area. One elder said, "We may not live to see these trees grow, but our grandchildren will."

That moment was a powerful reminder that respect for the planet is respect for the future. By teaching children the importance of sustainability, we plant seeds of peace for generations to come.

Lesson: Environmental respect is an investment in global peace and prosperity.

5. Respect in Technology: Ethical Innovation
In the digital age, respect must extend to how we develop and use technology. Ethical innovation prioritizes privacy, equity, and accessibility, ensuring

that technological advancements serve humanity rather than harm it.

Anecdote: Digital Inclusion

In a remote village, I introduced a digital literacy program for women who had never touched a computer. One participant, a widow named Layla, learned to use email to reconnect with her son, who was studying abroad.

Layla said, "I thought technology wasn't for people like me. Now I see it can bring us closer."

By respecting their right to access technology, we empowered these women to participate in the digital world and strengthened their connections with loved ones.

Lesson: Respect in technology ensures that progress benefits everyone, not just a privileged few.

A Call to Action: Building a Culture of Respect

As I conclude this book, I leave you with a call to action: let us make respect the foundation of our lives and our world.

The Power of Respect

To policymakers: Respect your people by crafting laws that protect their dignity and rights. Respect other nations by pursuing diplomacy over conflict.

To educators: Teach respect not as a passive value but as an active practice. Show students how to listen, empathize, and appreciate diversity.

To parents: Model respect in your homes. Children learn from what they see, and your actions will shape their worldview.

To individuals: Practice respect in your daily interactions. Speak with kindness, act with patience, and listen with an open heart.

The Power of Respect: Building Bridges to Peace and Human Dignity

Respect is a cornerstone of peace and a gateway to human dignity. It fosters understanding, builds connections, and creates pathways for harmony among individuals and communities. The Universal Declaration of Human Rights (UDHR), as adopted and proclaimed by the United Nations General Assembly in Resolution 217 A (III) on December 10, 1948, stands as a testament to this principle. This illustrated booklet highlights key articles from the

The Power of Respect

UDHR, underscoring the universal values that uphold human rights and dignity across cultures and nations. Through respect, we honor these shared ideals, bridging divides and fostering a world rooted in equity and compassion.

Here's a rewritten and polished version for your book:

Call to Action: Understanding and Living the 30 Articles of Human Rights
Now is the time to embrace and learn the 30 Articles of Human Rights—a blueprint for understanding not only your own rights but also the rights of others. This knowledge is a foundation for building a safer, more peaceful world while fostering a sense of unity and shared humanity. Your presence, ideas, and enthusiasm are vital as we explore these essential topics: human rights, respect, communication, education, and the urgent need to teach the next generation—our children—their rights and responsibilities.

Through the "Channel for Unity and Gender", we are united in our mission to empower every individual to reclaim their dignity, independence, and respect. These are values that belong to every person by right, forming the foundation of human connection and progress. Today, we aim to ignite real actions that inspire meaningful change and build momentum for lasting progress.

The Path to Lasting Change: A Focus on the 30 Articles

The 30 Articles of Human Rights serve as a guidepost—a way to measure impact, exchange ideas, and empower each other to keep pushing for a better world. Below is our actionable framework for translating these principles into real-world change:

1. Education Initiatives

> *Empowerment Workshops:* Offer practical workshops to educate individuals about their rights, legal protections, and opportunities for leadership, employment, and active community participation.
>
> *Awareness Campaigns:* Launch focused campaigns addressing critical issues like gender equality, personal safety, and the importance of education—especially for girls and women.
>
> *Mentorship Programs:* Pair experienced mentors with individuals seeking guidance in their professional and personal growth.

2. Financial Independence

Financial Training Workshops: Organize sessions with experts to teach essential skills such as budgeting, financial management, and small-business development.

Entrepreneurship Programs: Provide step-by-step guidance for launching sustainable businesses, with a focus on accessible resources and innovative, low-cost startup ideas.

Skill Development: Train individuals in high-demand skills to increase opportunities for meaningful employment.

3. Housing Advocacy

Collaborations with Local Organizations: Partner with housing initiatives to secure safe and affordable living spaces, especially for single mothers, survivors of domestic violence, and vulnerable communities.

Shelter Access: Compile and share a directory of emergency shelters and housing options for those in urgent need.

4. Community Engagement

>*Events and Celebrations:* Host community gatherings to share success stories, promote initiatives, and rally support for human rights advocacy.

>*Social Media Campaigns:* Use digital platforms to amplify messages, educate the public, and build networks to support gender equality and empowerment.

5. Feedback and Progress Tracking

>Regularly attend discussions to evaluate progress, celebrate milestones, address challenges, and refine action plans to ensure continuous improvement.

Your Role in This Movement
Every action matters, and there are countless ways to contribute to this shared vision:

>*Share Resources:* Connect us with organizations, individuals, or initiatives aligned with our mission to maximize collective impact.

The Power of Respect

Volunteer: Bring your skills and time to specific projects, such as leading workshops, designing campaign materials, or organizing events.

Spread the Word: Use your networks to promote this cause, inviting others to join and contribute to the change.

Empowering Humanity: A Collective Responsibility

This is more than a discussion—it's about action. By empowering individuals, particularly women, with the tools for financial independence, education, and advocacy, we create the foundation for a future where everyone thrives—not just survives.

We envision a world where every person:

Knows their rights and has the tools to defend them.

Possesses the confidence to lead, learn, and succeed.

Has access to the resources needed for a life free from dependency, poverty, and fear.

The Power of Respect

Together, we can bring this vision to life. Your voice, ideas, and involvement are crucial. Reach out with your thoughts, suggestions, or offers of support through Instagram or other platforms. Every effort counts, and together, we can create a world where human rights are universally upheld, empowering every individual to lead a life of dignity, respect, and independence.

Let's take this journey together—starting today! By learning the 30 article.

🌎 Free and Equal - Article 1

The Power of Respect

All Human Beings Are Born Free and Equal: A Call for Unity and Action

The very first article of the Universal Declaration of Human Rights (UDHR) proclaims a profound and universal truth: "All human beings are born free and equal in dignity and rights." This foundational principle reminds us that, regardless of race, gender, religion, nationality, or any other distinction, we are united by our shared humanity. Each person deserves respect, compassion, and the freedom to live with dignity.

The idea of equality is not just a moral ideal—it is essential for building a peaceful and just world. When we act with reason and compassion and treat one another as equals, we foster communities where everyone can thrive. This spirit of brotherhood is the foundation of cooperation, mutual respect, and global unity.

Unfortunately, the reality often falls short of this ideal. Discrimination, inequality, and prejudice still plague our world. A stark example is the apartheid system in South Africa, which enforced racial segregation and denied basic rights to the majority Black population. The system dehumanized millions, treating them as inferior based solely on the color of their skin. It took

The Power of Respect

decades of resistance, led by figures like Nelson Mandela, to dismantle this unjust system and begin the journey toward equality.

Another example is the gender inequality faced by women worldwide. From unequal pay to limited access to education, women are often denied the same opportunities as men. Malala Yousafzai's story exemplifies the fight for gender equality. After surviving an attack by extremists for advocating for girls' education, Malala has become a global symbol of resilience and the importance of treating all people equally, regardless of gender.

While challenges persist, progress is possible when we embrace the principles of equality and unity. Movements for civil rights, gender equality, and LGBTQ+ rights show that change happens when people come together to demand justice and fairness.

As individuals, we have a role to play. By cooperating for peace, advocating for kindness, and spreading unity, we contribute to a world where equality becomes a reality. Treating others with dignity and respect isn't just an obligation—it's the foundation for a brighter, more inclusive future.

The Power of Respect

Let's honor the principle that all human beings are born free and equal, working together to create a world where everyone's humanity is respected, and no one is left behind.

No Discrimination - Article 2

🌍 Article 2: No Discrimination—Upholding Equality for All

Article 2 of the Universal Declaration of Human Rights proclaims that everyone is entitled to all the

The Power of Respect

rights and freedoms set forth in the declaration, without discrimination of any kind. It asserts that characteristics such as race, religion, gender, language, political opinion, or social status should never determine a person's worth or opportunities. This principle stands as a cornerstone for equality, dignity, and justice in a world too often divided by prejudice and bias.

Discrimination erodes the very fabric of society, creating barriers that deny individuals their basic rights and freedoms. It limits opportunities, marginalizes communities, and steals hope, dignity, and freedom from those affected. Whether it occurs in education, employment, healthcare, or housing, discrimination divides humanity, fostering resentment and conflict.

A stark real-world example is the systemic racial segregation and discrimination of Black Americans under Jim Crow laws in the United States. For decades, Black individuals were denied equal access to education, jobs, and public spaces. The laws perpetuated inequality, forcing millions to endure poverty and social exclusion. The Civil Rights Movement, led by figures like Martin Luther King Jr., was a direct response to this injustice, highlighting the

The Power of Respect

need to dismantle discriminatory practices and uphold Article 2's principles.

Another example is the treatment of the Rohingya people in Myanmar. This Muslim minority group has faced decades of discrimination and persecution, denied citizenship and basic rights solely because of their religion and ethnicity. In 2017, these discriminatory policies escalated into violence, forcing hundreds of thousands to flee their homes. This tragic situation demonstrates how unchecked discrimination can escalate into severe human rights abuses.

Eliminating discrimination requires collective effort. As individuals, we can speak out against prejudice, treat everyone with respect, and advocate for policies that promote equality. Governments and institutions must enforce anti-discrimination laws, promote inclusion, and address systemic biases that perpetuate inequality.

By honoring Article 2, we affirm our commitment to a world where everyone belongs—a world where opportunities are not dictated by race, religion, gender, or any other characteristic but by the shared humanity that unites us all. Together, we can build a future where equality is not just an aspiration but a reality for all.

The Power of Respect

You Have a Right to Life - Article 3

🌏 Article 3: The Right to Life—A Universal Promise

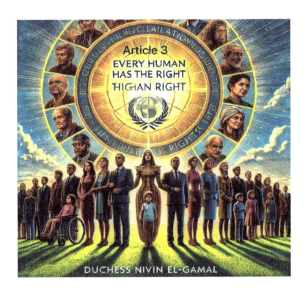

Article 3 of the Universal Declaration of Human Rights declares that everyone has the right to life, liberty, and security. This right ensures that every individual—child or adult—can live with dignity, free from fear, violence, or deprivation. It is a cornerstone of all human rights, as life is the foundation upon which liberty, security, and all other rights are built.

The Power of Respect

The right to life means more than mere survival; it encompasses the opportunity to thrive. Every child deserves access to love, education, healthcare, and a safe environment to grow. Depriving someone of this right is not just a violation of their dignity—it robs them of their potential and undermines the progress of humanity as a whole.

A tragic example of this right being denied is seen in the ongoing conflict in Syria. Millions of children have grown up in the shadow of war, facing bombings, displacement, and a lack of access to basic necessities like food, shelter, and education. These children, robbed of security and stability, are unable to enjoy the simple joys of childhood or dream of a brighter future.

Another powerful example is the story of Malala Yousafzai, who was targeted and shot by extremists in Pakistan for advocating for girls' education. Denying girls the right to education is a direct attack on their right to life and dignity, as it limits their potential and reinforces cycles of poverty and inequality. Despite the violence she faced, Malala survived and became a global advocate for children's rights, proving that resilience and hope can triumph over adversity.

The Power of Respect

To honor Article 3, we must act collectively to ensure every individual, especially children, can live in safety and with opportunity. Supporting organizations that provide healthcare, education, and protection for vulnerable populations is a critical step. Advocacy against violence, poverty, and discrimination also helps create an environment where every child has a chance to thrive.

Every individual has a role to play in upholding the right to life. By standing against injustice, fostering equal opportunities, and promoting peace, we can create a world where every child can grow, dream, and contribute to a better future. Together, we can turn the promise of Article 3 into a reality for all.

The Power of Respect

You cannot be enslaved - Article 4

🌍 Stand Against Slavery and Humiliation: Upholding Freedom and Dignity

Article 4 of the Universal Declaration of Human Rights unequivocally states that no one shall be held in slavery or servitude. It is a powerful reminder that slavery, in any form—whether physical, emotional, or social—has no place in our world. Despite this declaration, modern slavery continues to affect

The Power of Respect

millions of people globally, robbing them of their freedom and dignity.

Modern slavery takes many forms, including human trafficking, forced labor, and domestic servitude. A glaring example is the plight of domestic workers in the Gulf region and other parts of the world. Many maids, nannies, and housekeepers endure grueling work schedules of 18 to 20 hours a day, with only a few hours of sleep. Their passports are confiscated, stripping them of their autonomy and leaving them vulnerable to verbal, physical, and emotional abuse. Threats of deportation and further punishment keep them silent, trapped in a cycle of exploitation.

This form of servitude highlights how modern slavery persists under the guise of employment, violating fundamental human rights. Governments, organizations, and individuals must work together to eradicate this exploitation by holding employers accountable, enforcing strict labor laws, and providing resources to protect these workers.

One inspiring example of collective action took place in India in 2018. A small community rallied to free 20 workers trapped in bonded labor at a brick kiln. Through education, legal action, and collaboration with local organizations, they secured the workers'

The Power of Respect

freedom and ensured that justice was served. This case shows the power of grassroots efforts in combating slavery and restoring dignity to those who have been dehumanized.

To stand against slavery and humiliation, we must educate ourselves about its modern forms, support organizations fighting against exploitation, and advocate for fair treatment and justice. Being conscious consumers, choosing ethical brands, and reporting suspicious activity are also vital steps in this fight.

Slavery is not just a historical atrocity—it is a present-day crisis that demands immediate action. By raising our voices and taking a stand, we can break the chains of oppression and create a world where freedom and dignity are universal rights, not privileges. Together, we can fulfill the promise of Article 4 and ensure that no one lives in chains.

The Power of Respect

You Cannot Be Torture - Article 5

🌍 No One Deserves Torture: Upholding Dignity and Humanity

Article 5 of the Universal Declaration of Human Rights declares: "No one shall be subjected to torture or to cruel, inhuman, or degrading treatment or punishment." This article is a cornerstone of human dignity, asserting that cruelty has no place in any society. Torture dehumanizes not only the victim but also the perpetrator, eroding the moral fabric of communities and nations.

The Power of Respect

Torture is used to instill fear, suppress dissent, and strip individuals of their humanity. It violates fundamental principles of justice, compassion, and respect for human rights. A world where Article 5 is fully respected is one where people can live free from fear and oppression, where human dignity is prioritized, and where justice prevails.

A powerful example of the importance of this article can be seen in the story of Amal, a survivor of systemic torture. Amal was detained in her home country for expressing dissent against an oppressive regime. During her imprisonment, she endured inhumane treatment designed to break her spirit and silence her voice. Yet, Amal emerged resilient, dedicating her life to advocating for survivors of torture and promoting human rights. Her work has helped countless individuals reclaim their dignity and rebuild their lives, showing the transformative power of compassion and justice.

Unfortunately, despite the clear prohibition against torture, it remains a pervasive problem in many parts of the world. From political prisoners subjected to inhumane conditions to civilians tortured during conflicts, these abuses highlight the ongoing struggle to uphold Article 5. Governments, organizations, and individuals must work tirelessly to eradicate torture by

The Power of Respect

holding perpetrators accountable and supporting victims in their recovery.

To ensure this right is upheld globally, we must advocate for stronger legal frameworks, transparency, and international cooperation. Supporting organizations that document and combat torture, such as Amnesty International and the United Nations' Anti-Torture Initiative, is crucial. Public awareness campaigns and education can also help foster a culture of compassion and justice, making torture universally unacceptable.

By standing against torture, we affirm the inherent dignity of every individual. Let us commit to a world where no one suffers cruelty, and every person is treated with the humanity they deserve. Together, we can make the promise of Article 5 a reality for all.

The Power of Respect

🌍 Your Rights Remain No Matter Where You Are! - Article 6

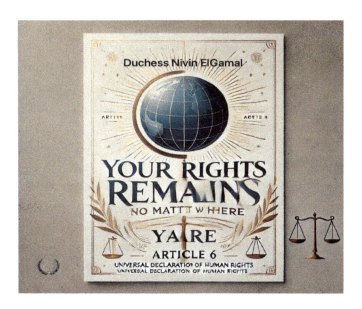

Article 6 of the Universal Declaration of Human Rights declares: "Everyone has the right to recognition everywhere as a person before the law." This powerful statement emphasizes that human rights are universal and indivisible, transcending borders, circumstances, and identities. Wherever you are in the world, your humanity and dignity must be acknowledged and protected.

The Power of Respect

This article is the cornerstone of equality and justice. It ensures that every individual is seen and treated as a person with inherent rights, regardless of their nationality, immigration status, or circumstances. Recognition before the law is not just a legal concept—it is a profound affirmation of human worth and dignity. Without this recognition, individuals are vulnerable to discrimination, exploitation, and injustice.

One tragic example of the violation of Article 6 is the plight of stateless individuals. Stateless people, such as the Rohingya in Myanmar, are denied recognition as citizens by any country. Without legal recognition, they are left without access to basic rights, including education, healthcare, and protection under the law. Their lack of status often subjects them to exploitation, forced displacement, and violence.

Similarly, migrants and refugees often face challenges in asserting their rights in foreign countries. They may be treated as invisible by legal systems, denied access to fair treatment, and left unprotected against abuse. For instance, many Syrian refugees have struggled to gain recognition and legal protection in host countries, leaving them vulnerable to exploitation and unable to rebuild their lives.

The Power of Respect

Upholding Article 6 requires collective action. Governments must implement policies that ensure all individuals are recognized and protected under the law, regardless of their status or origin. Advocacy for stateless populations, refugees, and marginalized communities is essential to prevent these groups from falling through the cracks.

As individuals, we can champion the principles of this article by treating everyone with respect and advocating for policies that promote inclusion and equality. Supporting organizations that work to protect the rights of migrants, refugees, and stateless individuals is another meaningful way to contribute.

Let us commit to building a world where every person is valued and recognized, no matter where they are. Together, we can ensure that the universal promise of Article 6 becomes a reality for all.

The Power of Respect

Before The Law, We Are All Equal - Article 7

🌍 We Are All Equal Before the Law: The Fight for Justice and Dignity

Article 7 of the Universal Declaration of Human Rights affirms: "All are equal before the law and are entitled without any discrimination to equal protection of the law." This principle is a cornerstone of justice, ensuring that everyone, regardless of race, religion, gender, or status, is treated with fairness and dignity under the law.

The Power of Respect

Equality before the law is not just a legal requirement—it is a profound moral imperative that upholds the values of justice and human rights. When this principle is violated, societies fracture, perpetuating inequality, discrimination, and marginalization.

A striking example of the fight for equality comes from John Howard Griffin, an American journalist and social activist. In the late 1950s, Griffin, who was white, temporarily altered his skin color through medication and exposure to ultraviolet light to experience life as a Black man in the racially segregated American South. His journey, chronicled in his groundbreaking book Black Like Me, revealed the harsh realities of systemic racism.

Griffin endured humiliation, rejection, and even threats to his safety simply because of the color of his skin. His experiment exposed the stark inequality that existed in a society where the legal system often failed to protect Black individuals from discrimination and violence. Griffin's courageous work became a powerful catalyst for conversations about racial justice and the urgent need to uphold the principle of equality before the law.

The Power of Respect

Today, the lessons from Griffin's experience remain relevant. Injustice persists when legal systems fail to protect everyone equally. Racial profiling, gender discrimination, and unequal access to justice are just some of the ways inequality manifests globally.

To honor Article 7, we must actively challenge these injustices. Governments must enforce laws that protect all individuals equally, without bias or favoritism. Educational initiatives can help dismantle prejudices, while grassroots movements and advocacy campaigns ensure marginalized voices are heard.

As individuals, we can contribute by standing against discrimination in all its forms, promoting inclusive policies, and supporting organizations that fight for equality.

Equality before the law is not just a legal right—it is the foundation of a just and compassionate society. Together, we can build a world where every person's dignity and humanity are respected, protected, and celebrated.

The Power of Respect

Our Human Rights Are All Protected By Law - Article 8

🌐 Article 8: Human Rights—Our Shield and Foundation

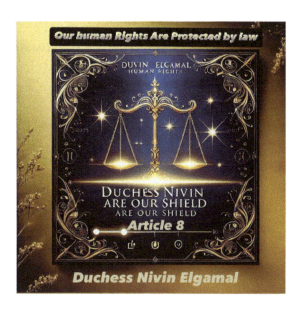

Human rights are the cornerstone of equality, justice, and dignity, safeguarded under the law to ensure that no one is left powerless in the face of injustice. Article 8 of the Universal Declaration of Human Rights affirms: "Everyone has the right to an effective remedy by competent tribunals for acts violating their fundamental rights." This principle guarantees that individuals have access to justice and the opportunity to seek redress when their rights are violated.

Article 8 stands as a shield for those facing discrimination, oppression, or unfair treatment. It ensures that justice is not a privilege but a universal right available to all, regardless of their background or circumstances. This article serves as a beacon of hope, reminding us that fairness and accountability must prevail in every society.

A powerful real-world application of Article 8 is its role in addressing injustices faced by marginalized communities. For instance, when individuals or groups experience unlawful discrimination, such as being denied equal opportunities in education, housing, or employment, Article 8 empowers them to challenge these violations in court. This framework reinforces accountability and strengthens the legal systems that uphold justice for all.

On a personal level, Article 8 played a pivotal role in my immigration journey to the United Kingdom. When faced with challenges that could have undermined my rights and dignity, I turned to this principle for protection and advocacy. The right to seek an effective remedy through competent legal channels ensured that my case was heard fairly and

The Power of Respect

justly. It was through this process that I was able to gain my UK citizenship, a testament to the power of human rights as both a shield and a foundation for a better future.

However, realizing the full potential of Article 8 requires vigilance and collective effort. We must advocate for strong legal systems that are accessible, transparent, and fair. We must also support those who lack the resources or knowledge to defend their rights, ensuring that no one is left behind.

By defending and upholding Article 8, we reinforce the values of equality, fairness, and human dignity. Let us stand united, championing justice and inspiring change so that these rights become a living reality for all.

The Power of Respect

You Cannot Be Unreasonably Detained – Article 9

🌎 Article 9: Freedom is a Fundamental Right No Unreasonable Detention

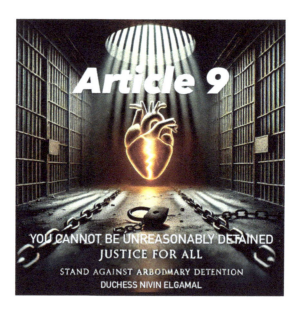

Article 9 of the Universal Declaration of Human Rights asserts: "No one shall be subjected to arbitrary arrest, detention, or exile." This article enshrines freedom as the cornerstone of justice, protecting individuals from unjust imprisonment and ensuring their dignity and equality. When this right is violated, the consequences ripple through families, communities, and societies, eroding trust in systems meant to uphold justice.

Freedom from arbitrary detention is vital for preserving human dignity. It ensures that no individual is detained without valid reason, legal process, or accountability. Arbitrary detention strips individuals of their liberty, silences dissent, and often leads to abuses of power. Upholding this right is essential to maintaining the balance of justice and fairness in society.

A tragic example of the violation of Article 9 is the case of Cao Shunli, a Chinese human rights activist. In 2011, Cao was arbitrarily detained for her efforts to advocate for government transparency and public participation in human rights matters. Held without due process, Cao was denied proper medical care despite her rapidly deteriorating health. Repeated pleas for medical attention were ignored, leading to her death from organ failure in custody in 2014.

Cao's story underscores the devastating consequences of arbitrary detention. Her death sparked international outrage, shining a light on the human cost of such violations and the urgent need for global accountability. Her case serves as a solemn reminder that freedom and justice must be protected for all, and

The Power of Respect

that no one should face persecution for advocating for their rights or the rights of others.

When arbitrary detention occurs, it threatens the very foundation of justice and freedom. It sends a message that power can override fairness and that individual rights are expendable. Such practices have no place in a just and equitable society.

To uphold Article 9, we must advocate for transparency, accountability, and strong legal frameworks that protect individuals from abuse. It is our collective responsibility to ensure that governments and institutions respect the rule of law and safeguard liberty for all.

Together, we can stand against injustice and inspire others to protect the fundamental right to freedom. By doing so, we honor the values of dignity, fairness, and equality that unite us all.

The Power of Respect

You Have The Right To A Fair Trial- Article 10

📣 Justice for All: Article 10—The Right to a Fair Trial ⚖️

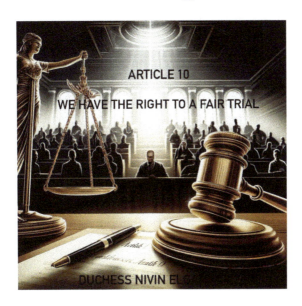

Article 10 of the Universal Declaration of Human Rights guarantees everyone the right to a fair and public hearing by an independent and impartial tribunal. This principle is a cornerstone of justice, ensuring accountability, protecting the vulnerable, and upholding the rule of law. A fair trial is essential for maintaining trust in legal systems and ensuring that no one, regardless of their status or power, is above the

The Power of Respect

law. Sadly, violations of this principle are far too common. For instance, some individuals abuse their power as trustees, exploiting the trust placed in them to misuse funds or assets meant for vulnerable individuals, such as children. These acts of fraud not only violate the law but also erode the very foundation of justice and trust.

I personally experienced such injustice when Altaf Noorani, a Supreme Court lawyer in the UK acting for the UAE Embassy, misused my son's trust funds. He diverted the funds for personal gain, allowing the money's interest to disappear and even attempted to conceal more than one attempt on our lives. Such crimes, rooted in exploitation and greed, highlight the urgent need for transparency, accountability, and fair trials to ensure justice prevails.

Globally, fraudulent trustees face serious legal consequences. In the United States, convictions for such crimes can result in up to 20 years in prison, particularly in cases involving significant financial losses or vulnerable victims. In the United Kingdom, the Fraud Act 2006 provides for up to 10 years of imprisonment, along with heavy fines and restitution orders. These penalties not only seek to punish but also deter others from committing similar offenses.

The Power of Respect

To uphold Article 10, trials must be conducted with integrity and impartiality. Judges take an oath to uphold the law and act with fairness, ensuring that truth and justice prevail over wealth and influence.

Consider the story of Adam, an honest man facing a trial against James, a powerful individual with immense financial resources. Adam's struggle is emblematic of countless others who face systemic inequality. It is the sacred duty of judges to honor their oath, ensuring that fairness is upheld and that justice serves all, not just the wealthy or powerful.

Let us stand for a world where fairness, truth, and justice triumph over corruption and influence, honoring the rights and dignity of every individual.

You Are Innocent Until Proven Guilty - Article 11

🌏 Article 11: You Are Innocent Until Proven Guilty—A Cornerstone of Justice

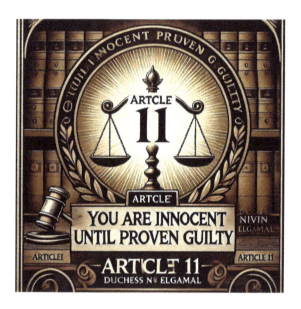

Article 11 of the Universal Declaration of Human Rights establishes a vital principle of justice: "Everyone charged with a penal offense has the right to be presumed innocent until proved guilty according to law in a public trial at which they have had all the guarantees necessary for their defense." This principle safeguards individuals from prejudice and premature

The Power of Respect

judgment, ensuring that justice is served fairly and impartially.

The presumption of innocence is not just a legal concept—it is a fundamental human right. Without it, individuals risk having their lives torn apart based on accusations alone. It ensures that everyone is given the opportunity to defend themselves and that guilt must be established through evidence, not assumption.

A glaring example of the consequences of disregarding this principle is the case of Richard Jewell. In 1996, Jewell was a security guard at the Summer Olympics in Atlanta, Georgia, who discovered a suspicious backpack containing a bomb and helped save countless lives. However, he soon became the prime suspect in the bombing, largely due to speculation and media frenzy.

Although Jewell was never charged and was eventually exonerated, the damage was already done. The media and public labeled him guilty before any evidence was presented. His reputation was destroyed, his career derailed, and his peace of mind shattered. Jewell's case is a stark reminder of the devastating effects of presuming guilt and the critical importance of upholding Article 11.

The Power of Respect

When individuals are presumed guilty without proof, it undermines trust in legal systems and violates basic human rights. It not only punishes the innocent but also weakens the principle of fairness that underpins justice.

To uphold Article 11, we must ensure that trials are conducted impartially, free from public and media bias, and that accused individuals are treated with dignity and respect until proven guilty. Public awareness campaigns, judicial training, and responsible media practices can all help reinforce this principle.

Justice must prevail, and presuming innocence is key to maintaining fairness, equality, and trust in our global community. Let us stand together to protect this fundamental right, ensuring that everyone has the chance to defend themselves and live free from premature judgment.

The Power of Respect

You Have A Right To Privacy - Article 12

🌐 **Celebrating 2025: Your Right to Privacy – Article 12**

As 2025 begins, I celebrate the completion of this book and reflect on the principles that bind us together as one human family. Among these is the universal right to privacy, protected under Article 12 of the Universal Declaration of Human Rights. This article states: "No one shall be subjected to arbitrary interference with his privacy, family, home, or correspondence, nor to attacks upon his honor and reputation."

Privacy is more than a personal preference—it is a fundamental human right that safeguards our dignity, freedom, and individuality. It grants us the space to live authentically, free from unnecessary scrutiny or judgment. In an era defined by technological advancements and interconnected lives, the right to privacy is more relevant than ever.

Imagine a world where privacy is disregarded—where personal conversations are monitored, homes invaded without cause, and reputations destroyed by false claims. Such violations strip away not only security but also the essence of human dignity. Protecting privacy is not just about securing data or personal information; it is about honoring the sacred boundaries of our lives.

A stark reminder of the importance of Article 12 lies in the increasing instances of digital privacy breaches. From unauthorized surveillance to cyber-attacks that expose sensitive information, these violations demonstrate the urgent need for stronger protections. For instance, whistleblowers like Edward Snowden highlighted how unchecked surveillance can erode the

The Power of Respect

fundamental right to privacy, sparking global conversations on accountability and transparency.

As we step into 2025, let us pledge to uphold and respect this essential right—not only for ourselves but for everyone. Governments must enact and enforce robust privacy laws, technology companies must prioritize user security, and individuals must remain vigilant in protecting their personal lives. Together, we can create a world where privacy is valued, dignity is preserved, and freedom flourishes.

This book is a testament to the enduring power of human rights and the belief that we are born free and equal. As we celebrate this new year, may it bring peace, joy, and compassion into your life. Let us honor our shared humanity and work toward a brighter, safer, and more just world.

Here's to a united 2025, where privacy and dignity remain at the heart of our global community.

The Power of Respect

You Have Freedom To Move - Article 13

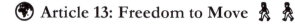 Article 13: Freedom to Move

Article 13 of the Universal Declaration of Human Rights guarantees the right to freedom of movement, stating: "Everyone has the right to move freely within their country, to choose their residence, to leave any country—including their own—and to return at will." This fundamental freedom is a cornerstone of human dignity, enabling individuals to seek safety, opportunity, and connection.

The Power of Respect

Freedom of movement empowers people to shape their lives, whether by pursuing education, building careers, reuniting with loved ones, or escaping danger. It ensures that borders do not become barriers to dignity and growth. Without this right, individuals face limitations that stifle their potential and infringe upon their humanity.

Consider the story of Maria, a young professional who grew up in a country with severe restrictions on movement. She was denied opportunities to study abroad or access global career prospects. For years, she felt trapped, her dreams confined by invisible walls. However, when Maria finally moved to a country that respected Article 13, her life transformed. She studied at a prestigious university, found meaningful work, and built a future filled with opportunity. Her experience underscores the profound impact of freedom of movement in unlocking human potential.

This right also plays a critical role in protecting refugees fleeing conflict or persecution. Millions rely on the ability to cross borders to seek safety for themselves and their families. Freedom of movement ensures they can escape harm, find refuge, and, when conditions allow, return home to rebuild their lives.

The Power of Respect

However, this right is under threat in many parts of the world. Political restrictions, discriminatory policies, and closed borders often deny individuals the ability to move freely. Such limitations not only harm individuals but also hinder global progress by restricting the flow of talent, ideas, and cultural exchange.

To honor Article 13, governments must uphold the right to move freely, providing legal frameworks that respect this freedom. As individuals, we can support refugees, advocate for inclusive immigration policies, and challenge unjust restrictions on movement.

Freedom of movement is not just about physical relocation—it is about accessing a life of dignity, choice, and possibility. Let us stand united to protect this fundamental right for all, ensuring that borders never limit the human spirit.

The Power of Respect

You Have The Right To Seek A Safe Place To Live - Article 14

🌍 The Right to Seek Safety

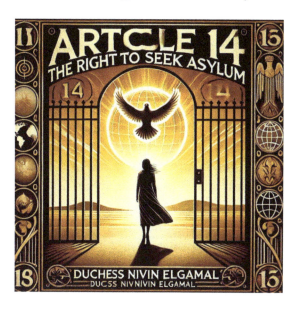

Article 14 of the Universal Declaration of Human Rights asserts: "Everyone has the right to seek and to enjoy in other countries asylum from persecution." This fundamental right provides hope and protection for those fleeing violence, war, or oppression, ensuring they can rebuild their lives in safety and dignity.

The Power of Respect

Seeking asylum is not about privilege; it is about survival and the preservation of fundamental human rights. Millions around the world rely on this right to escape life-threatening situations and find a safe haven where they can start anew.

A compelling example of the importance of this right is the story of Malala Yousafzai, a Nobel laureate and global advocate for education and women's rights. In 2012, Malala was targeted and shot by the Taliban in Pakistan for her outspoken commitment to girls' education. Her survival was miraculous, but remaining in her home country was no longer safe. Malala and her family sought asylum in the United Kingdom, where she recovered and continued her advocacy work. The right to asylum not only saved her life but also empowered her to become a global force for justice and equality.

For countless others, asylum offers a lifeline. Refugees fleeing war-torn regions, political dissidents escaping persecution, and victims of systemic violence rely on the promise of safety that Article 14 provides. However, the journey to asylum is often fraught with challenges. Refugees face dangerous travel, hostile policies, and the stigma of displacement.

The Power of Respect

To uphold Article 14, we must advocate for compassionate and inclusive asylum policies. Governments have a moral and legal obligation to ensure that those seeking refuge are treated with dignity, not suspicion or hostility. Communities can support this effort by welcoming refugees and providing resources to help them rebuild their lives.

Asylum is not just a legal right; it is a testament to humanity's shared commitment to protect the vulnerable. When we honor this right, we affirm the values of compassion, justice, and global unity.

Let us stand together to ensure that the right to seek safety remains a beacon of hope for all who need it. By doing so, we help build a world where every individual can live in peace and dignity.

The Power of Respect

🌐 Articles 13 & 14: Freedom to Move and Seek a Safe Place to Live

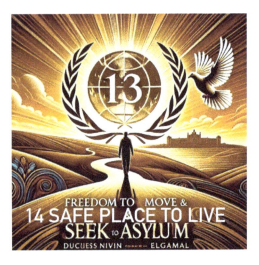

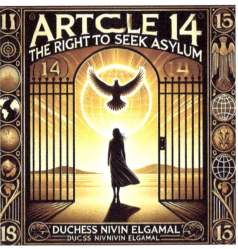

The Power of Respect

Freedom of movement and the right to seek asylum are fundamental to human dignity and justice. These rights, enshrined in Articles 13 and 14 of the Universal Declaration of Human Rights, affirm that every individual has the right to move freely and find refuge from persecution. Together, they form a framework that ensures the freedom to live, move, and seek safety with dignity.

Article 13 guarantees that everyone has the right to move freely within their country, choose their residence, and leave any country—including their own—and return whenever they choose. This right recognizes the importance of mobility in seeking better opportunities, reuniting with loved ones, or escaping danger.

Article 14 builds on this principle by ensuring the right to seek and enjoy asylum in other countries when fleeing persecution. For many, this right offers a lifeline, allowing them to escape violence, oppression, or war and rebuild their lives in safety.

These rights must be upheld with fairness and compassion. Restrictions on movement or asylum should be necessary and proportionate, ensuring no one is unjustly harmed. Governments and societies have a shared responsibility to protect these freedoms, ensuring that borders do not become barriers to safety and dignity.

A powerful example of these rights in action is the story of Malala Yousafzai, the Nobel laureate and global advocate for education and women's rights. After surviving an assassination attempt by the Taliban in Pakistan, Malala and her family sought asylum in the United Kingdom. The right to asylum not only saved her life but also empowered her to continue her vital work on a global stage, advocating for millions of girls denied education.

At the same time, the plight of refugees and displaced persons around the world highlights the urgent need to uphold these rights. From Syrian families seeking safety from war to individuals fleeing political persecution, freedom of movement and asylum are essential for preserving lives and protecting human dignity.

As we reflect on Articles 13 and 14, let us commit to creating a world where everyone's rights are respected. Together, we can ensure that freedom, dignity, and safety are universal, offering hope to those seeking a better life.

The Power of Respect

You Have The Right To A Nationality - Article 15

🌐 Article 15: The Right to a Nationality 📜

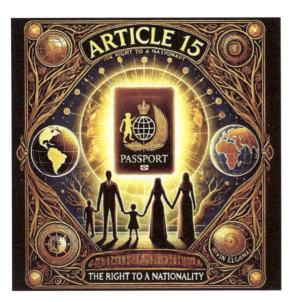

Article 15 of the Universal Declaration of Human Rights affirms that everyone has the right to a nationality and identity. This right guarantees that individuals belong to a nation, can obtain a passport, and cannot be arbitrarily deprived of their nationality. It also protects the right to change nationality and ensures that every child inherits their parents'

nationality, preserving their history, heritage, and sense of belonging.

Nationality is more than a legal status—it is a vital connection to one's roots, identity, and opportunities. It provides access to fundamental rights such as education, healthcare, and the ability to travel, vote, and participate in society. Without nationality, individuals are rendered stateless, often excluded from opportunities and denied their dignity and basic rights.

An example of the challenges surrounding this right is the case of children born to parents of different nationalities. Imagine a child whose parents come from two different countries, but one parent denies the child their rightful nationality. This action erases part of the child's history, cutting them off from half of their cultural identity, heritage, and familial connections. Such denial can also restrict access to education, healthcare, and opportunities, leaving the child in limbo and vulnerable to exclusion and discrimination.

The plight of the Rohingya people further highlights the significance of Article 15. In Myanmar, the Rohingya were stripped of their citizenship, rendering them stateless. Without nationality, they lost access to education, healthcare, and legal protections, making them vulnerable to persecution and forced displacement. This tragic situation underscores the importance of safeguarding the right to nationality for all.

To uphold Article 15, governments must ensure that nationality laws are inclusive, equitable, and respect the rights of individuals. Legal frameworks should protect against arbitrary deprivation of nationality and recognize the importance of heritage and identity. Communities and organizations must also advocate for those who are stateless or at risk of losing their nationality, ensuring their rights are restored.

Nationality is not just about a passport—it is about belonging, identity, and the ability to build a future. Let us work together to protect this fundamental right, ensuring that everyone has the chance to thrive and connect to their heritage and humanity.

The Power of Respect

You Have The Right To Form A Family- Article 16
🌍 Article 16: The Right to Form a Family— "Marriage and Family"

Article 16 of the Universal Declaration of Human Rights ensures that every adult has the right to marry and establish a family, regardless of race, nationality, or religion. This fundamental right emphasizes equality in marriage and family life, protecting individuals from discrimination and ensuring that unions are based on the free and full consent of both parties. It recognizes the family as the cornerstone of society, deserving of protection by both society and the state.

Marriage is a profound bond that transcends cultural and national boundaries, uniting individuals in love, mutual respect, and shared purpose. Article 16 safeguards the integrity of this institution, affirming that every person has the right to choose their partner freely and equally, without interference or coercion.

An inspiring example of this principle in action is the story of Omar and Jumana, who came from different cultural and religious backgrounds. Despite societal pressures and expectations, they exercised their right to marry freely and with mutual consent. Their union symbolizes the essence of Article 16—love and understanding beyond racial, national, and religious divides. Their story reminds us that the strength of a family lies in mutual respect, compassion, and shared values, not in external labels or boundaries.

The family, as the fundamental unit of society, plays a crucial role in fostering stability, nurturing future generations, and promoting social harmony. Philosopher Will Durant once said, "The family is the nucleus of civilization." This highlights the vital role

The Power of Respect

families play in shaping communities and preserving cultural and moral values.

However, around the world, many individuals are denied the right to marry or form families due to restrictive laws, cultural biases, or societal pressures. Forced marriages, discrimination based on race or religion, and unequal treatment in family laws are violations of this right that must be addressed.

To uphold Article 16, societies and governments must ensure that marriage is based on consent, equality, and respect. Legal frameworks should protect individuals from discrimination and coercion, while promoting the well-being and security of families.

Let us celebrate and protect the right to form a family, recognizing its importance in building a just, inclusive, and compassionate world. Together, we can ensure that every individual's right to love and belong is respected and upheld.

The Power of Respect

You Have The Rights To Own Property - Article 17

🌐 Article 17: The Right to Own Property

Article 17 of the Universal Declaration of Human Rights establishes that everyone has the right to own property, individually or in association with others, and that no one shall be arbitrarily deprived of their property. This principle affirms that property ownership is a fundamental right and emphasizes the responsibility of property owners, trustees, and the state to ensure safety, fairness, and compliance with legal standards.

Property is more than a possession; it represents security, stability, and an opportunity to build a life.

The Power of Respect

However, as Martin Luther King Jr. aptly said, "Property is intended to serve life." Its value lies in how it contributes to human dignity and well-being, not in the accumulation of material wealth.

One example of this principle in action involves tenants and landlords. Consider a tenant living in an apartment with hazardous conditions, such as faulty wiring or unsafe plumbing. The landlord is legally obligated to address such issues promptly, ensuring the property is habitable and safe. Failure to do so not only violates legal standards but also risks the tenant's safety and well-being. Legal consequences for noncompliance can include fines, liability for damages, or even loss of property ownership rights.

Another example involves eminent domain, where governments sometimes seize private property for public use. While this can be lawful, it must be done fairly, with proper compensation and adherence to due process. Arbitrary or unjust seizures violate Article 17 and undermine trust between individuals and governing bodies.

Globally, challenges persist in upholding property rights. In some regions, individuals are forcibly evicted without fair compensation, leaving families without homes or livelihoods. Corruption,

The Power of Respect

discriminatory practices, and neglect often exacerbate these issues, particularly for vulnerable populations.

To protect the right to own property, it is essential to enforce laws that safeguard individuals from arbitrary deprivation and ensure that all properties meet safety and habitability standards. Landlords, architects, and property owners must comply with regulations designed to protect occupants, while governments must uphold transparency and fairness in property-related matters.

By honoring Article 17, we affirm that property is a tool to support human dignity and a foundation for stability and opportunity. Together, we can create a world where property ownership is fair, just, and accessible to all.

The Power of Respect

Freedom of Thought, Conscience And Religion- Article 18

🌐 Article 18: Freedom of Thought, Conscience, and Religion

Freedom is Our Birthright

Article 18 of the Universal Declaration of Human Rights is a profound acknowledgment of our shared humanity and the inherent right of every individual to freedom of thought, conscience, and religion. This fundamental right safeguards the essence of personal

The Power of Respect

beliefs and ensures that everyone can live in alignment with their values and faith without fear of oppression or judgment.

What Article 18 Protects:
- The freedom to choose, practice, or change your religion or beliefs.
- The right to express your beliefs alone or with others, in public or private.
- The ability to manifest your beliefs through teaching, worship, practice, or observance.

Freedom of thought and religion is a cornerstone of peace and diversity in society. It allows us to celebrate our differences and recognize the universal truths that unite us. For me, as Duchess Nivin El-Gamal, this right is deeply personal. I affirm my belief as a Muslim in one God and the messengers who were sent to deliver His divine message, culminating in Islam—'Peace.' This belief reminds us of our shared purpose: to foster harmony, respect, and understanding among all people.

However, Article 18 also calls on us to refrain from judgment. As human beings, we must respect each other's beliefs and choices, acknowledging that the role of ultimate judgment belongs to God alone. To impose our will on others' faith or practices violates the very principle of freedom and equality that Article 18 upholds.

An Example of Courage and Freedom:
Think of Malala Yousafzai, who stood up for her right to education—a manifestation of her belief in equality and justice—even when faced with violence and oppression. Her story demonstrates the power of freedom of thought and conscience to inspire change and build a better world.

🌿 **Embracing Diversity and Peace:**
Let us honor Article 18 by respecting each other's faiths and beliefs, fostering understanding, and building bridges of compassion. Freedom of thought and religion enriches our world, creating a society where everyone can live their truth and worship in peace.

Together, we can uphold this fundamental right and create a future where diversity is celebrated, and unity prevails.

The Power of Respect

Freedom to Express Opinions - Article 19

🌍 The Power of Free Expression

Article 19 of the Universal Declaration of Human Rights asserts: "Everyone has the right to freedom of opinion and expression." This fundamental right ensures that individuals can hold opinions without interference and seek, receive, and share information through any media, regardless of borders. It is a cornerstone of democracy, empowering individuals to express themselves freely and fostering creativity, innovation, and progress.

The Power of Respect

✨ What Article 19 Protects:
- The freedom to hold opinions without fear or interference.
- The ability to share ideas and information across any platform, transcending borders and barriers.

Freedom of expression is the engine of open dialogue and accountability in society. It enables journalists to report truthfully, activists to advocate for justice, and ordinary people to share their stories, perspectives, and beliefs. This right drives the pursuit of truth and encourages societies to evolve through transparency and inclusion.

Freedom in Action:
Consider Greta Thunberg, a young activist who has used her voice to advocate for urgent climate action. Through speeches, social media, and global platforms, she has inspired millions to take a stand for the planet. Her fearless expression of her opinions exemplifies the transformative power of Article 19 in addressing critical global issues and fostering change.

Similarly, journalists and whistleblowers worldwide risk their safety to expose corruption, injustice, and abuse of power. Their work underscores the necessity of protecting freedom of expression, ensuring that truth prevails and that governments and institutions are held accountable.

Challenges to Article 19:
Despite its importance, this right is often under threat. In many regions, individuals face censorship, imprisonment, or violence for expressing their views. Restrictive laws, online surveillance, and media suppression undermine the very essence of freedom of expression, silencing voices that challenge injustice or question authority.

❦ Let Us Protect This Right:
To uphold Article 19, we must stand against censorship, advocate for press freedom, and ensure that everyone has the opportunity to share their perspectives without fear. By defending this right, we promote a world where every voice matters, diversity is celebrated, and progress thrives.

Freedom of expression is not just a right—it is a responsibility to use our voices to inspire change and create a more just and inclusive world.

The Power of Respect

Freedom To Join Groups- Article 20

Standing Up for Freedom of Assembly:
🌐 Article 20 of the Universal Declaration of Human Rights

Article 20 of the Universal Declaration of Human Rights (UDHR) embodies a fundamental principle: the right to freedom of peaceful assembly and association. It declares that every individual has the right to gather with others for a cause they believe in and the equally important right to refrain from joining groups or associations against their will. This article protects both individual autonomy and collective freedom, ensuring that no one is compelled into unwanted alliances or coerced into groups under duress.

This principle is especially crucial in contexts where people's ability to freely associate is undermined. For instance, in war-torn regions, countless individuals have been forced into associations that strip away their freedom and humanity. A poignant example is the plight of child soldiers, who are coerced into militias, robbed of their innocence, and manipulated to serve violent causes. These violations not only harm the individuals directly involved but also leave lasting scars on families and entire communities.

A specific and harrowing violation of Article 20 occurred under ISIS, where individuals, including children, were forcibly recruited into the organization through threats, violence, and manipulation. Young boys were trained as child soldiers, and civilians were compelled to adopt the group's ideologies, often at great personal and familial cost. Such coercion exemplifies why the right to freedom of assembly and association must be upheld. It is a safeguard against exploitation and a defense of human dignity.

The Power of Respect

The importance of Article 20 extends beyond protection from forced associations. It also empowers individuals to unite for shared purposes, advocate for justice, and build solidarity in peaceful movements. From grassroots campaigns to global initiatives, the freedom to gather and associate is the foundation of societal progress and democratic engagement.

As we reflect on Article 20, it is essential to reaffirm our commitment to its principles. Upholding the right to choose one's associations freely and rejecting forced alliances is a collective responsibility. By protecting this right, we safeguard not only individual freedom but also the integrity of communities and the prospect of a peaceful, equitable world.

Let us stand firm in defending the right to assemble and associate freely, ensuring that every person can live without fear of coercion and with the full dignity they deserve.

The Power of Respect

You Have The Right To Democracy - Article 21

🌍 Empowering Participation: Article 21 and the Right to Shape Society

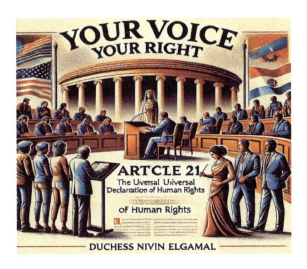

Article 21 of the Universal Declaration of Human Rights (UDHR) enshrines a fundamental principle of democracy: the right of every individual to participate in the government of their country, either directly or through freely chosen representatives. This article underscores the transformative power of active civic engagement, ensuring that every voice has a chance to influence the decisions that shape society.

The Power of Respect

At its core, Article 21 guarantees several key rights: the ability to vote, to run for public office, and to engage with decision-makers. These rights are not mere privileges reserved for the few; they are the bedrock of equality and representation in any society. By empowering individuals to participate in governance, this article fosters accountability, transparency, and inclusivity within political systems. It ensures that no one is excluded from the decision-making process due to their background, beliefs, or circumstances.

The right to participate is not just a tool for shaping policies—it is a mechanism for building fairness and justice. When people are given a voice in their government, they are more likely to trust its institutions and abide by its laws. Democratic participation strengthens the social contract, creating a society where citizens feel empowered to advocate for their needs and aspirations.

As someone actively involved in politics, I have witnessed the profound impact of participation. I have seen communities transformed when individuals exercise their right to vote or step forward as leaders to represent their people. This engagement often leads to meaningful change, as policies and decisions better reflect the diverse needs of the population. However,

The Power of Respect

this right is also a responsibility. Each of us must recognize our role in ensuring the fairness and integrity of the systems that allow us to participate. By voting, running for office, or engaging in dialogue with leaders, we contribute to the ongoing pursuit of justice and equality.

Yet, in many parts of the world, barriers to participation persist. Voter suppression, corruption, and systemic inequalities undermine the spirit of Article 21. It is our collective duty to dismantle these obstacles and uphold the principle that every voice matters.

In honoring Article 21, we affirm the universal right to participate in governance and strengthen the foundation of a fair and just society—one where every individual has a hand in shaping their future.

The Power of Respect

You Have The Right To Social Security- Article 22

🌐 Upholding Dignity: Article 22 and the Right to Social Security

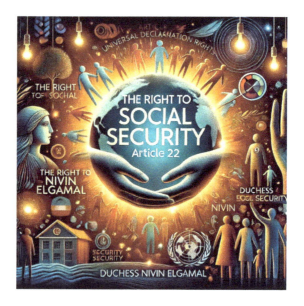

Article 22 of the Universal Declaration of Human Rights (UDHR) asserts that everyone has the right to social security, recognizing the vital role of systems designed to safeguard dignity and well-being. This right ensures that individuals have access to support during times of need, enabling them to lead lives of dignity while contributing to their communities. It

The Power of Respect

reflects a collective responsibility to foster economic, social, and cultural development, creating a fairer and more equitable society for all.

At its essence, social security guarantees that no one is left to struggle alone in the face of hardship. Whether through healthcare, unemployment benefits, pensions, or housing support, these systems form the backbone of a society that values its citizens and prioritizes their well-being. Social security not only addresses immediate needs but also helps empower individuals to achieve their potential, contributing to societal progress.

A powerful example of this principle in action is the National Health Service (NHS) in the United Kingdom. Established in 1945, the NHS was founded on the principle that healthcare should be available to everyone, regardless of financial circumstances. By providing free medical care, the NHS has ensured that millions of people receive essential treatments without fear of financial ruin. It is a testament to the transformative power of collective responsibility in guaranteeing human dignity.

On a global scale, the Copenhagen Declaration on Social Development further emphasizes the importance of social security. This landmark

The Power of Respect

agreement calls for universal social protection, the eradication of poverty, and the pursuit of full employment. By advocating for robust social safety nets, the declaration underscores the shared responsibility of nations to ensure that every individual has the opportunity to thrive.

These examples highlight how social security systems uphold the ideals of Article 22, ensuring that individuals are not only protected during times of need but also provided the means to lead fulfilling lives. They remind us that a just society is one that actively invests in its people, fostering resilience and equity.

In honoring the spirit of Article 22, we recognize the profound importance of social security in building a world where every person's dignity and well-being are safeguarded, empowering individuals to contribute to a thriving, inclusive global community.

The Power of Respect

You Have The Right To Work -
🌍 Article 23 The Right to Work: Upholding Dignity and Equality

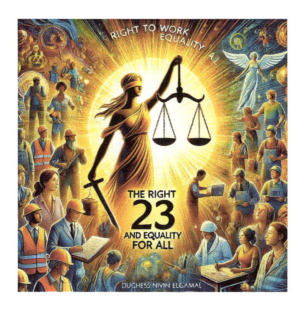

Article 23 of the Universal Declaration of Human Rights (UDHR) enshrines the fundamental right to work, emphasizing free choice of employment, fair working conditions, and protection against unemployment. It advocates for equal pay for equal work, regardless of race, gender, or other factors, and stresses the importance of inclusion for all, including individuals with disabilities. This right is not just about economic survival; it is about fostering dignity,

The Power of Respect

independence, and a sense of purpose for every individual.

Work is a cornerstone of human dignity. It allows people to support themselves and their families while contributing to the development of their communities. However, barriers such as discrimination, systemic inequality, and restrictive immigration policies often strip individuals of this right, denying them the opportunity to lead fulfilling lives. For instance, individuals with disabilities frequently face exclusion from the workforce, despite possessing the skills and capabilities to contribute meaningfully.

A poignant example of the denial of this right is the case of Nasrin Sotoudeh, an Iranian human rights lawyer and advocate. Despite her qualifications and dedication to justice, Sotoudeh faced severe barriers to practicing law due to her work in defending marginalized groups and promoting equality. Her case underscores how discrimination not only impacts an individual's livelihood but also erodes their independence and silences their voice.

The denial of the right to work reverberates far beyond the individual. It weakens communities, perpetuates inequality, and stifles economic growth.

The Power of Respect

Upholding the principles of Article 23 requires more than legislation—it demands proactive measures to create inclusive workplaces, eliminate discrimination, and provide fair opportunities for all.

Efforts to promote this right are critical for building just societies. Policies that ensure equal pay, protect workers from exploitation, and provide job security are essential. Furthermore, initiatives to support marginalized groups, including individuals with disabilities and immigrants, are necessary to ensure that everyone can access meaningful employment opportunities.

In championing Article 23, we affirm the value of every individual and the importance of work in fostering self-worth and societal progress. A just society is one that guarantees not only the right to work but also the conditions that allow everyone to thrive with dignity, equality, and respect.

The Power of Respect

You Have The Right To Rest And Time Off- Article 24

🌍 The Right to Rest: Embracing Renewal and Balance

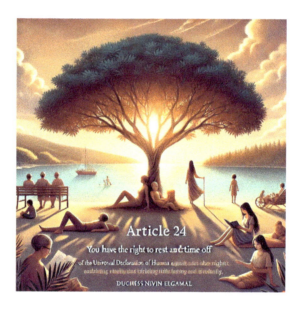

Article 24 of the Universal Declaration of Human Rights declares that everyone has the right to rest and leisure, including reasonable working hours and regular holidays. This fundamental right is a reminder that rest is not a luxury but a necessity for physical, emotional, and mental well-being. It acknowledges

The Power of Respect

the importance of stepping away from the demands of daily life to restore energy, focus, and productivity.

In a world that often glorifies constant activity, taking time to recharge can feel like an indulgence. Yet, honoring this right is essential for living a balanced and fulfilling life. Rest allows us to reflect, heal, and grow, equipping us to navigate life's challenges with renewed strength. As the saying goes, "You cannot pour from an empty cup." To help others and fulfill our responsibilities, we must first care for ourselves.

This principle resonated deeply during a transformative chapter in my life. After enduring a whirlwind of highs and lows, I realized the importance of stepping back to prioritize my well-being. For months, I embraced a season of retreat—what I called my "hermit mode"—to rebuild, reflect, and heal. In that quiet space, I found peace, rediscovered my purpose, and gained the resilience to rise above judgment and adversity.

Rest is not a sign of weakness or laziness; it is a powerful act of self-respect and preservation. By giving ourselves permission to pause, we create room for clarity, creativity, and connection. This renewal enables us to step into the next season of life with strength and confidence, ready to shine and inspire others.

The right to rest also honors the cyclical nature of life. Just as the seasons shift, so do our needs and priorities. Embracing these changes allows us to find balance, adapt to new circumstances, and emerge stronger.

As I reflect on my journey, I am grateful for the lessons learned and the people—both supportive and challenging—who shaped my path. Resting and recharging have made it possible to embrace new beginnings with hope, purpose, and light.

Let us honor Article 24 by prioritizing rest, cherishing the seasons of life, and recognizing that taking time for ourselves is not just a right but a profound gift that enriches our journey and the lives of those around us.

The Power of Respect

You Have The Right To Food & Shelter - Article 25

🌍 The Right to Food and Shelter: A Foundation for Dignity and Security

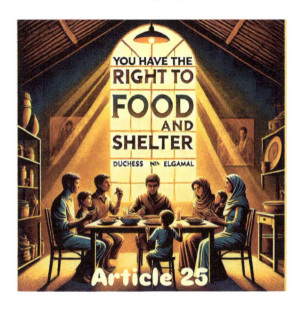

Article 25 of the Universal Declaration of Human Rights affirms that everyone has the right to a standard of living adequate for their health and well-being, including access to food, clothing, housing, and medical care. This essential right is the foundation of human dignity, ensuring that no one should endure the pain of hunger or the fear of homelessness. It is a reminder that basic needs are not privileges—they are fundamental to life itself.

Food and shelter are more than physical necessities; they are sources of security, stability, and hope. They provide the foundation for individuals and families to build meaningful lives, pursue their dreams, and contribute to their communities. When people are deprived of these basic needs, they are not only denied physical sustenance but also the opportunity to thrive.

Reflecting on this right, I think of the countless individuals whose resilience shines in the face of adversity. Their stories highlight the profound impact that access to food and shelter has on one's ability to heal, grow, and move forward. For example, during times of personal hardship, it was the stability of a safe home and the nourishment of shared meals that provided me with the strength to overcome challenges. These essentials became anchors, grounding me in hope and possibility.

Yet, for many around the world, these basic rights remain out of reach. Homelessness, food insecurity, and poverty continue to strip people of their dignity and opportunities. This reality calls on us to take collective action, ensuring that everyone has access to the essentials that sustain life. Initiatives such as food

The Power of Respect

banks, affordable housing programs, and community kitchens exemplify the power of compassion and shared responsibility in addressing these urgent needs.

Honoring Article 25 means more than meeting immediate needs; it means building a world where no one is left behind. It is about creating systems that ensure everyone, regardless of their circumstances, can live with dignity and security.

As I reflect on the importance of this right, I am reminded of the resilience and humanity that bind us all. Providing food and shelter is not just about survival—it is about offering hope, stability, and the chance for a brighter future. Let us commit to upholding this right for everyone, fostering a world where dignity and opportunity are within reach for all.

The Power of Respect

You Have The Right To Education- Article 26

🌐 The Right to Education: Unlocking Potential and Promoting Peace

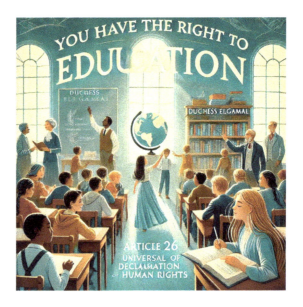

Article 26 of the Universal Declaration of Human Rights establishes the right to education as a universal principle, stating that elementary education should be free and accessible to all. Education is more than just a means of acquiring knowledge; it is a transformative tool for personal development, fostering equality, and promoting peace and understanding among nations, cultures, and religions.

The Power of Respect

Education plays a crucial role in shaping individuals and societies. It equips people with the skills they need to build meaningful lives, make informed decisions, and contribute to their communities. Furthermore, education fosters tolerance, understanding, and respect for diversity, serving as a cornerstone for global peace and cooperation.

Despite its recognized importance, many individuals worldwide are denied access to education. A striking example of this is the case of Malala Yousafzai, a Pakistani activist who was shot by the Taliban for advocating for girls' education. In her region, cultural norms and extremist ideologies sought to strip girls of their right to learn, leaving them vulnerable and marginalized. Malala's bravery brought global attention to the millions of children, especially girls, who are deprived of education due to poverty, gender discrimination, conflict, and oppressive policies.

The denial of education has far-reaching consequences. Without education, individuals are often trapped in cycles of poverty, unable to access opportunities for better livelihoods. Societies suffer as well, losing out on the potential contributions of educated citizens who could drive innovation, economic growth, and social progress.

The Power of Respect

Education should be a right, not a privilege. Governments and communities must work together to remove barriers such as poverty, discrimination, and systemic inequalities that prevent children from accessing schools. Parents, too, have a responsibility to ensure their children receive an education. Denying a child the chance to learn should be considered a grave violation of their rights. For instance, a parent who deliberately keeps their child out of school, whether due to neglect or harmful ideologies, should face legal consequences, as this deprives the child of their fundamental right to education and a brighter future.

By upholding the principles of Article 26, we invest in a more just, equitable, and peaceful world. Education is the key to unlocking potential, breaking down barriers, and fostering a global community rooted in understanding, tolerance, and respect for all.

Let's unite to ensure education for all—because an educated world is a foundation for peace, equality, and progress. Respect and understanding flourish through education, forming the cornerstone of harmony and mutual dignity. Respect is the bridge that connects us across differences and the pillar that upholds our shared humanity, fostering a future where everyone thrives together.

The Power of Respect

You Have The Right To Your Own Creations - Article 27

🌐 The Right to Your Own Creations: Protecting Innovation and Cultural Expression

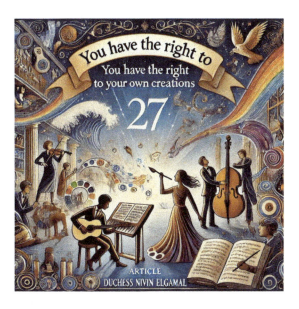

Article 27 of the Universal Declaration of Human Rights affirms the right of every individual to freely participate in the cultural life of their community, enjoy the arts, and share in scientific advancements and their benefits. It also guarantees the protection of the moral and material interests resulting from one's scientific, literary, or artistic creations. This article

The Power of Respect

celebrates human creativity and innovation, ensuring that individuals can contribute to and benefit from cultural and intellectual progress.

The right to your own creations is not just about protecting intellectual property; it is about fostering an environment where creativity thrives, ideas flourish, and diverse voices are celebrated. This right empowers inventors, artists, scientists, and thinkers to explore their potential, share their contributions, and receive recognition and reward for their efforts.

Consider the story of Steve Jobs and the creation of the iPhone. Jobs' innovative vision revolutionized communication and transformed modern life. Article 27 protects not only his right to develop this invention but also ensures that society can benefit from it. Similarly, artists like Frida Kahlo, whose deeply personal and cultural works have inspired millions, have their creations safeguarded under this principle, allowing their legacy to endure while respecting their authorship.

Unfortunately, violations of this right often occur, such as the theft of indigenous knowledge or cultural artifacts without proper acknowledgment or benefit-sharing. For instance, traditional medicinal practices developed by indigenous communities have been

The Power of Respect

commercialized by corporations without fair compensation or credit to the original creators. This exploitation undermines the spirit of Article 27, highlighting the need for robust protections.

Protecting the right to one's creations is vital for promoting innovation and preserving cultural heritage. It encourages individuals to invest time, energy, and resources into their pursuits, knowing their work will be respected and their contributions valued. At the same time, this right ensures that society benefits from these creations, fostering a cycle of progress and enrichment.

As a creator myself, I have experienced the profound satisfaction of seeing my ideas come to life and contribute to the world. Whether through art, invention, or writing, the ability to share one's creations and receive recognition is a cornerstone of personal fulfillment and societal advancement.

Let us honor Article 27 by protecting and celebrating creativity in all its forms, ensuring that every individual has the freedom and opportunity to contribute to the ever-evolving tapestry of human culture and progress.

Article 27 of the Universal Declaration of Human Rights says:

The Power of Respect

- You have the right to freely participate in cultural life, enjoy the arts, and share in scientific progress.
- Your creative works, whether scientific, literary, or artistic, are protected from theft and misuse.

Real-Life Example:
In the tech world, Nikola Tesla's groundbreaking innovations were often overshadowed or exploited. For instance, Thomas Edison is widely credited for inventions that Tesla's work significantly contributed to, such as advancements in electrical systems. Tesla's lack of recognition during his time serves as a reminder of the importance of protecting creators and giving credit where it's due.

Why it matters:
Protecting creators ensures that innovation and cultural contributions thrive. Every invention, painting, book, or song shapes our world—and the people behind them deserve respect, recognition, and reward.

Celebrate creativity and stand against idea theft. Together, we can build a future that values and protects human ingenuity.

You Have the Right To A Fair & Free World - Article 28

🌐 The Right to a Fair and Free World: Building a Just Global Society

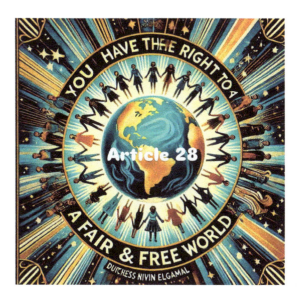

Article 28 of the Universal Declaration of Human Rights states that everyone is entitled to a social and international order in which the rights and freedoms outlined in the declaration can be fully realized. This article underscores the importance of creating systems—both societal and global—that uphold justice, equality, and human dignity. It emphasizes the collective responsibility of governments, institutions,

The Power of Respect

and individuals to foster a fair and free world where human rights are universally respected.

A fair and free world is more than an ideal—it is a necessity for global peace and progress. When societies are governed by fairness, individuals can live without fear of discrimination, oppression, or exploitation. Internationally, a fair world ensures that nations collaborate to address pressing issues like poverty, inequality, and conflict, fostering a global community rooted in mutual respect and shared responsibility.

Unfortunately, the abuse of this right is evident in many instances where social and international systems fail to uphold justice. One stark example is the ongoing Rohingya crisis in Myanmar. The Rohingya, a Muslim minority group, have faced decades of systemic discrimination, violence, and forced displacement. The social and international order in their case has failed to protect their rights, leaving them vulnerable to persecution and statelessness. Despite international laws and conventions meant to safeguard human rights, the lack of enforcement and global accountability has perpetuated their suffering.

Another example is the exploitation of vulnerable workers in global supply chains. Many laborers in

The Power of Respect

developing countries work under inhumane conditions, with little to no protection of their rights. Multinational corporations often prioritize profits over the welfare of workers, exploiting weak regulatory systems and perpetuating cycles of poverty and inequality.

To uphold Article 28, governments must work together to strengthen international frameworks that promote fairness and justice. This includes enforcing human rights laws, holding perpetrators accountable, and addressing systemic inequalities. On a societal level, fostering inclusivity, combating discrimination, and ensuring equal opportunities are essential steps toward creating fair systems.

The right to a fair and free world is not just a lofty goal—it is a call to action. By addressing the failures and abuses of social and international systems, we can work toward a world where every individual's rights and freedoms are fully realized, building a future rooted in justice, equality, and shared humanity.

Real-Life Example:
The Rohingya crisis in Myanmar highlights the failure of social and international systems to protect human rights. Decades of discrimination and violence have

The Power of Respect

left the Rohingya stateless and persecuted, showing why we must strengthen global accountability.

Why it matters:
A fair and free world isn't just a dream—it's a responsibility. Together, we can dismantle systems of inequality, hold violators accountable, and create a global community rooted in justice and peace.

Let's work for a world where EVERYONE's rights are upheld.

The Power of Respect

You Have a Responsibility to Respect Other People's Rights - Article 29

🌍 The Responsibility to Respect Others' Rights: Balancing Freedom with Accountability

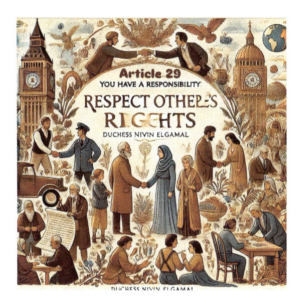

Article 29 of the Universal Declaration of Human Rights underscores the vital balance between enjoying one's own rights and respecting the rights of others. It states that everyone has duties to their community, as it is within this collective framework that individuals can fully realize their potential and freedoms. While individual rights are fundamental, they must be exercised in a way that respects the rights and well-being of others and adheres to the principles of morality, public order, and the greater good in a democratic society.

This article serves as a reminder that freedom is not absolute; it comes with responsibilities. Rights such as freedom of expression, assembly, and religion are essential, but their misuse to harm others or incite violence contradicts the very principles of human rights. This balance ensures a harmonious society where all individuals can coexist peacefully while contributing to the collective good.

A powerful real-world example of the abuse of this principle is seen in the context of hate speech. Hate speech, often disguised as freedom of expression, has caused significant harm to communities worldwide. A tragic example is the Rwandan Genocide in 1994, where hate speech and propaganda, particularly through media outlets like Radio Télévision Libre des Mille Collines (RTLM), incited violence and fueled mass atrocities. The misuse of the right to free speech led to devastating consequences, underscoring the importance of limiting rights when they infringe on others' dignity and safety.

The Power of Respect

On the other hand, respecting this responsibility can lead to remarkable societal progress. For instance, when communities embrace inclusivity and reject discrimination, they foster environments where all individuals can thrive. This is evident in countries like Canada, which has implemented strong anti-discrimination laws and multicultural policies to ensure that individual freedoms do not come at the expense of others' rights.

Respecting others' rights is not just a legal obligation; it is a moral duty that underpins the fabric of a fair and democratic society. It calls on individuals to act responsibly, balancing their personal freedoms with the collective well-being of their community.

By adhering to Article 29, we honor the interconnected nature of our rights and responsibilities, ensuring that our actions contribute to a world where freedom, respect, and equality are upheld for all.

The Power of Respect

Our Human Rights Shall Not Be Taken Away - Article 30

🌍 Our Human Rights Shall Not Be Taken Away: Upholding Dignity and Humanity

Article 30 of the Universal Declaration of Human Rights serves as a powerful safeguard, ensuring that no one, whether a person, group, or institution, can engage in actions or policies that strip individuals of their rights and freedoms. It emphasizes the inviolability of human rights, asserting that these

The Power of Respect

fundamental rights are universal and must be protected under all circumstances.

The core of this article lies in preserving human dignity. Dignity is the foundation of human rights—it is what gives every individual their intrinsic worth. When rights are stripped away, it is not just freedoms that are lost, but also the very essence of humanity. To deny someone their rights is to deny their dignity, reducing them to mere objects of control, oppression, or violence.

A harrowing real-world example of dignity being stripped away is the story of Nelson Mandela during apartheid in South Africa. For 27 years, Mandela was imprisoned for opposing a regime that institutionalized racial segregation and denied basic rights to the majority of its population. While in prison, Mandela endured inhumane treatment, harsh labor, and the constant attempt to break his spirit. The apartheid system did not just seek to control the Black population—it sought to dehumanize them, stripping away their dignity and reducing them to second-class citizens in their own land.

Yet Mandela's story also demonstrates the resilience of the human spirit. Despite the attempts to strip him of his humanity, he emerged from imprisonment with his dignity intact and led a movement that transformed his country. His unwavering commitment to justice and reconciliation serves as a testament to the power of human dignity, even in the face of systematic efforts to erase it.

The importance of Article 30 cannot be overstated. It is a reminder that human rights are non-negotiable and that no person or authority has the legitimacy to undermine them. It reinforces the idea that the destruction of rights anywhere threatens humanity everywhere.

By honoring this article, we affirm the universality and indivisibility of human rights, safeguarding dignity and humanity for all. It is our collective responsibility to ensure that no one is stripped of their rights or their inherent worth, protecting the freedom and dignity of every individual.

Living the 30 Articles of Human Rights: A Path to Peace

As we conclude this chapter, it is important to reflect on the 30 Articles of the Universal Declaration of Human Rights (UDHR) and the profound impact they can have when embraced in our daily lives. These articles are more than just principles on paper; they are the foundation for a world rooted in respect, dignity, and equality. They provide a roadmap for understanding our own rights, respecting the rights of others, and fostering harmony in our relationships, communities, and societies.

The 30 Articles: A Framework for Peace

Each article of the UDHR plays a critical role in shaping a peaceful and just world. For example:

- Article 1, reminds us that all human beings are born free and equal in dignity and rights. This sets the tone for universal respect, regardless of nationality, race, or gender.
- Article 3, protects the right to life, liberty, and security of person, forming the basis for safety and freedom in society.
- Article 19, safeguards freedom of opinion and expression, enabling open dialogue and mutual understanding.
- Article 26, emphasizes the right to education, ensuring that every individual has the tools to thrive and contribute to their community.

When these rights are upheld, they create a ripple effect of fairness and understanding, laying the foundation for a world free from conflict and oppression.

The Power of Respect

Understanding Rights to Respect Boundaries
Learning the 30 Articles isn't just about knowing your own rights—it's about recognizing and respecting the rights of others. This awareness helps us set healthy boundaries in our personal and professional relationships, creating an environment where mutual respect flourishes. For example:

- Respecting Article 12, (freedom from arbitrary interference in privacy) helps us honor others' personal space and choices.
- Upholding Article 23, (the right to work in favorable conditions) ensures fair treatment in the workplace.
- Valuing Article 18, (freedom of thought, conscience, and religion) promotes inclusivity and acceptance of diverse beliefs.

When we honor these rights in our interactions, we foster trust, understanding, and cooperation—key ingredients for peaceful living.

A Life Shaped by the Articles
Imagine a world where the 30 Articles are embraced by all. This vision is not just aspirational—it is entirely achievable through education and action. A life shaped by these principles is one where:

The Power of Respect

1. Equality Prevails: No one is marginalized or excluded because of their race, gender, or beliefs.
2. Conflicts are Resolved Peacefully: Differences are addressed through dialogue, guided by mutual respect.
3. Opportunities are Shared: Everyone has access to education, work, and the resources they need to thrive.

This is the beautiful life the UDHR envisions, a life where every individual feels seen, heard, and valued.

The Role of Education
Education plays a pivotal role in bringing the 30 Articles to life. By teaching these rights to children and the next generation, we instill values of respect, empathy, and responsibility. Schools, community workshops, and public awareness campaigns can ensure that every individual understands their rights and the importance of respecting others'.

For example:
   - Article 26, which guarantees the right to education, not only empowers individuals with knowledge but also fosters a culture of lifelong learning and self-improvement.

The Power of Respect

- Article 27 (the right to participate in cultural life) encourages creativity and appreciation of diverse traditions, breaking down barriers between communities.

Education is the catalyst for turning these principles into actions, ensuring that respect and equality are passed on to future generations.

A Call to Action
Now that we've explored the 30 Articles, the responsibility lies with us to put them into practice. Here's how you can contribute:

1. Educate Yourself and Others: Share what you've learned about the 30 Articles with friends, family, and your community.
2. Advocate for Change: Stand up against injustices and support policies that uphold human rights.
3. Lead by Example: Treat others with dignity and fairness, reflecting the principles of the UDHR in your daily life.

By taking these steps, we can collectively build a world where human rights are not just ideals but lived realities.

The Power of Respect

A Peaceful World Begins with Us
The 30 Articles of Human Rights provide a framework for creating a world where peace, respect, and dignity prevail. When we learn to respect each other's boundaries and rights, we create an environment where everyone can thrive. This understanding transforms our relationships, strengthens our communities, and sets the stage for a future defined by harmony and compassion.

As we carry the lessons of this chapter forward, let us remember that change begins with each of us. By living these principles, we can create a world that is not only safer but also more beautiful—where every individual is free to live a life of dignity, respect, and purpose. Together, we can turn the vision of the Universal Declaration of Human Rights into a reality, one action at a time.

The Power of Respect

Chapter 8: United for Human Rights: Activities and Enrichment for Empowerment

Human rights are the foundation of dignity, freedom, and equality for all. This chapter is dedicated to uniting education with action, offering a series of enriching activities, lessons, and assignments designed to inspire learners to not only understand human rights but to become active participants in their defense and promotion.

Learning Objectives

By the end of this chapter, participants will:

- Understand the Universal Declaration of Human Rights (UDHR) and its relevance to modern youth.
- Recognize the importance of humanitarian actions and the power of individual contributions.

The Power of Respect

- Develop critical thinking through statistics and problem-solving assignments.
- Create projects and pledges to promote human rights awareness and advocacy in their communities.

1. Teaching Emphasis: Human Rights Overview

Begin the lesson by exploring the Universal Declaration of Human Rights (UDHR). Highlight its origins, principles, and significance. Key quotes from the UDHR can serve as thought-provoking discussion starters:

- "All human beings are born free and equal in dignity and rights."
- "Everyone has the right to education."
- "No one shall be subjected to torture or to cruel, inhuman, or degrading treatment."

Activity:

Divide learners into small groups and assign each a specific article of the UDHR. Have them:

- Analyze its meaning.
- Discuss its importance in today's context.
- Present their findings through a skit, poster, or digital presentation.

The Power of Respect

2. United Enrichment Activities

A. The "Learn United" Song

Music can be a powerful tool for unity and inspiration. Introduce a song that reflects the themes of human rights, or challenge participants to write their own lyrics that express the importance of freedom, equality, and justice.

Activity:

- Teach learners the song and discuss its message.
- Organize a performance to share the song with the broader community, such as during a school assembly or human rights awareness event.

B. United Paper Plan

A "United Paper Plan" serves as a blueprint for action. In this activity, learners will outline steps to address a specific human rights issue in their community or school.

The Power of Respect

Activity:

1. Identify a human rights issue (e.g., bullying, access to education, or homelessness).

2. Develop a plan with these components:

- **Problem Identification**: What is the issue?
- **Proposed Solution**: What actions can be taken?
- **Resources Needed**: What materials or support are required?
- **Timeline**: When will the plan be implemented?

3. Present the plan to a panel of peers, educators, or community leaders.

3. **Humanitarian Success Stories**

Inspire learners with real-life examples of individuals who have made significant contributions to human rights. Share the stories of:

- Malala Yousafzai's fight for girls' education.
- Nelson Mandela's leadership in ending apartheid.
- Eleanor Roosevelt's role in drafting the UDHR.

The Power of Respect

Activity:

Research Assignment: Assign learners to research a humanitarian leader of their choice and write a profile detailing their achievements and impact.

Creative Component: Encourage students to create a visual representation of their humanitarian's journey, such as a timeline or storyboard.

4. Independent Thinking Assignment: Human Rights in Action

Encourage learners to reflect on their own role in promoting human rights.

Prompt:

"Identify one human right that resonates with you. How can you defend or promote this right in your daily life? What challenges might you face, and how will you overcome them?"

5. Statistics Assignment: Understanding the Problem

To understand the scope of human rights issues, learners will analyze data related to topics such as poverty, access to education, or gender inequality.

The Power of Respect

Activity:

Provide students with statistical data (e.g., global literacy rates or child labor statistics). Ask them to:
- Interpret the data.
- Identify trends or disparities.
- Suggest solutions based on their analysis.

6. Problem and Solution: A Case Study Approach

Present a real-world human rights issue, such as the refugee crisis or climate change's impact on vulnerable populations.

Activity:
- Divide learners into teams and assign them a specific aspect of the issue.
- Each team will research, brainstorm solutions, and present their findings to the class.

7. The United Pledge for Human Rights

End the chapter by empowering learners to make a commitment to human rights. Create a pledge that reflects shared values and a united vision for a better world.

The Power of Respect

Sample Pledge:

"I pledge to uphold the principles of equality, justice, and freedom for all. I will stand against injustice and work towards creating a world where everyone's rights are respected and protected."

Activity:

- Have learners sign or personalize the pledge.
- Display the pledges as a *"Wall of Commitment"* in the classroom or community space.

8. Youth and the UDHR: Why It Matters

Close the chapter by revisiting the importance of the Universal Declaration of Human Rights, particularly for young people. Emphasize that the UDHR is not just a historical document but a living guide that empowers individuals to build a fair and just society.

Activity:

Ask learners to write a reflective essay or create a multimedia presentation answering the question:

"How can the UDHR inspire me to make a difference in my community?"

Conclusion

This chapter equips educators and learners with practical tools to explore, internalize, and act upon human rights principles. By blending knowledge with creativity, reflection, and action, we unite as a force for change, ensuring that the ideals of the UDHR live on in the hearts and hands of future generations.

Chapter 9: Combatting Human Trafficking: A Global Fight Against Exploitation

Human trafficking is one of the most pressing human rights violations in the world today, impacting millions of lives and undermining global progress towards justice and equality. This chapter provides an in-depth exploration of anti-human trafficking efforts, international legal frameworks, and practical approaches to understanding and addressing this complex issue.

Learning Objectives

By the end of this chapter, readers will:

- Understand the definition and scope of human trafficking and its distinction from smuggling.
- Explore the international legal instruments and frameworks designed to combat trafficking in persons.

- Examine the global and regional initiatives addressing human trafficking.
- Assess key challenges and solutions for combating trafficking at local, national, and international levels.

1. Definition of Trafficking in Persons

Human trafficking is defined under Article 3 of the **Protocol to Prevent, Suppress and Punish Trafficking in Persons**, supplementing the United Nations Convention Against Transnational Organized Crime (commonly referred to as the Palermo Protocol). It involves:

a) **Acts**: Recruitment, transportation, transfer, harboring, or receipt of persons.
b) **Means**: Threat or use of force, coercion, abduction, fraud, deception, abuse of power, or a position of vulnerability.
c) **Purpose**: Exploitation, which includes forced labor, sexual exploitation, slavery, servitude, or organ removal.

2. Trafficking vs. Smuggling of Migrants

It is crucial to distinguish between trafficking in persons and smuggling of migrants, as these terms are often conflated:

- Trafficking in Persons: Involves exploitation and can occur with or without the victim's consent. The defining element is the use of coercion or deception for exploitation.
- Smuggling of Migrants: A consensual act where individuals pay to be transported illegally across borders, without intent of exploitation after arrival.

3. The Issue of Consent

Consent becomes irrelevant in cases of trafficking if any of the means (coercion, fraud, deception) are used. For children under the age of 18, consent is irrelevant regardless of whether means are involved, as outlined by the Palermo Protocol.

4. International Legal Frameworks

A. The United Nations Convention Against Transnational Organized Crime (UNTOC)

Adopted by the UN General Assembly in 2000, the UNTOC is a landmark international instrument addressing organized crime. It is supported by three protocols, including:

- Protocol to Prevent, Suppress and Punish Trafficking in Persons, Especially Women and Children (Trafficking Protocol): Focuses on preventing trafficking, protecting victims, and prosecuting offenders.
- Protocol Against the Smuggling of Migrants by Land, Sea, and Air: Targets migrant smuggling.

B. **Key Provisions of the Trafficking Protocol**

1. **Prevention**: Raising awareness, addressing root causes, and promoting international cooperation.
2. **Protection**: Assisting and supporting victims of trafficking, ensuring they are not treated as criminals.
3. **Prosecution**: Criminalizing trafficking offenses and promoting international legal cooperation.

C. Other Relevant International Instruments

- ILO Forced Labour Conventions (No. 29 and No. 105): Address forced labor as a form of exploitation.
- Convention on the Rights of the Child (CRC): Protects children from exploitation.
- Convention on the Elimination of All Forms of Discrimination Against Women (CEDAW): Tackles trafficking of women for sexual exploitation.

5. Regional Frameworks and Initiatives

Regional cooperation is critical in combating trafficking. Examples include:

- European Union Directives: Sets minimum standards for identifying and supporting trafficking victims.
- African Union Plan of Action on Human Trafficking: Aims to strengthen regional responses.
- Association of Southeast Asian Nations (ASEAN): Promotes regional dialogue and collaboration.
- Organization of American States (OAS): Works on strengthening regional mechanisms.

6. Problem Assessment

A. The Scope of Human Trafficking

Trafficking is a global issue, with estimates from the International Labour Organization (ILO) indicating that over **27.6 million people** are in situations of forced labor or exploitation worldwide. Victims are often trafficked for:

- Sexual exploitation (majority of cases).
- Forced labor in industries like agriculture, construction, or domestic work.
- Organ removal.

B. Factors Contributing to Human Trafficking

1. **Economic Inequality**: Poverty and lack of economic opportunities make individuals vulnerable to trafficking.
2. **Conflicts and Displacement**: Refugees and internally displaced persons are at higher risk.
3. **Weak Legal Systems**: Insufficient enforcement of anti-trafficking laws.
4. **Demand**: For cheap labor and sexual exploitation fuels the trafficking industry.

C. Challenges in Combating Human Trafficking

1. **Identifying Victims**: Victims often fear reprisal or are unaware of their rights.

2. **Cross-Border Jurisdictions**: Trafficking networks operate across borders, complicating law enforcement efforts.

3. **Corruption**: Complicity of officials undermines anti-trafficking efforts.

7. Addressing the Problem: Solutions and Strategies

A. Strengthening International Cooperation

Global efforts like the Global Program Against Trafficking in Human Beings (GPAT) aim to assist governments in criminalizing and prosecuting trafficking cases. Key initiatives include:

- Developing regional task forces.
- Sharing intelligence and best practices.

B. Victim-Centered Approaches

Trafficking victims require specialized support, including:

- Legal assistance to protect their rights.

- Access to healthcare, counseling, and reintegration programs.
- Safe housing and employment opportunities.

C. Awareness and Education

- Public campaigns to inform communities about the risks of trafficking.
- Training for law enforcement, healthcare workers, and educators on identifying and assisting victims.

D. Enhanced Legal Frameworks

- Ratification and implementation of international instruments like the Palermo Protocol.
- Establishing harsher penalties for traffickers and intermediaries.

E. Data Collection and Research

Accurate data is essential for understanding trafficking trends and designing targeted interventions.

8. Case Studies: Implementing Solutions

Case Study 1: Regional Task Forces

The Southeast Asian Region developed cross-border task forces to combat trafficking, leading to increased prosecutions and better victim support.

Case Study 2: Technology Against Trafficking

Organizations like Tech Against Trafficking use data analytics and AI to track trafficking networks and rescue victims.

Conclusion

Human trafficking is a grave violation of human rights that requires collective action across nations, sectors, and communities. Through understanding the legal frameworks, addressing root causes, and empowering victims, we can combat this global menace and uphold the dignity and freedom of every individual.

The Power of Respect

Chapter 10: Respect Is Earned, Not Bought

Respect is one of the most fundamental pillars of human rights and social harmony. Unlike material possessions, respect cannot be purchased or coerced—it must be earned through actions, values, and the way we treat others. This final chapter explores the essence of respect as a cornerstone for individual character, relationships, and the broader pursuit of justice and equality. It challenges readers to reflect on their own behaviors and contributions to a world where respect is both given and received authentically.

Learning Objectives

- By the end of this chapter, readers will:
- Understand the true meaning of respect and its role in personal and societal contexts.
- Explore the relationship between respect and human rights.

- Identify ways to earn and give respect through values, actions, and integrity.
- Reflect on how fostering mutual respect contributes to social justice and equality.

1. What Does It Mean to Earn Respect?

Respect is not something owed; it is something cultivated through consistent effort and adherence to principles. It requires:

- **Integrity**: Staying true to your values and acting with honesty.
- **Empathy**: Understanding and valuing the perspectives and experiences of others.
- **Accountability**: Taking responsibility for your actions and their consequences.

Quote for Reflection

"Respect for ourselves guides our morals; respect for others guides our manners." – Laurence Sterne

2. Respect and Human Rights

Human rights and respect are deeply intertwined. Respect for individuals' dignity, freedoms, and equality forms the foundation of the Universal

The Power of Respect

Declaration of Human Rights. Without mutual respect, these rights cannot be upheld.

Key Points:

- Respect transcends differences such as race, gender, religion, or social status.
- Discrimination, prejudice, and inequality stem from a lack of respect for others' inherent worth.
- Upholding human rights begins with recognizing and respecting every individual's humanity.

Activity:

Encourage readers to examine scenarios where respect—or its absence—impacts human rights. For example:

- The way marginalized communities are treated in society.
- The importance of respecting refugees' rights and dignity.

The Power of Respect

3. Respect in Action: Building Bridges, Not Walls

Earning respect requires consistent effort in interactions with others. It involves:

- **Listening**: Being attentive to what others say and validating their feelings.
- **Fairness**: Treating everyone equally, regardless of their background or status.
- **Compassion**: Offering help and kindness without expecting anything in return.

Activity:

Ask readers to identify three ways they can show respect in their daily lives, such as:

- Resolving conflicts peacefully.
- Acknowledging the contributions of others.
- Standing up for someone whose rights are being violated.

4. Why Respect Cannot Be Bought

Material wealth or status may command attention, but they cannot substitute for genuine respect. Respect is earned through:

Character: Who you are when no one is watching.

The Power of Respect

Actions: How you treat people, especially those who can do nothing for you.

Consistency: Living in alignment with your principles every day.

Quote for Reflection

"You can demand fear or obedience, but true respect is freely given by those who see the good in you." – Unknown

5. Earning Respect in a Divided World

In today's world, divisions often arise due to misunderstandings, prejudice, or fear. Respect can serve as a bridge to overcome these barriers.

Steps to Foster Respect Across Differences:
1. **Educate Yourself**: Learn about other cultures, beliefs, and perspectives.
2. **Challenge Biases**: Confront stereotypes and prejudices, starting with your own.
3. **Lead by Example**: Show respect even in challenging situations, and inspire others to do the same.

6. Respect and Leadership

True leaders earn respect through service, humility, and dedication to the well-being of others. Leadership is not about authority but about influence built on trust and integrity.

Activity: Reflective Writing

Write about someone you respect deeply. What qualities make this person deserving of respect? How can these qualities be emulated?

7. The Role of Respect in Social Justice

Respect is a catalyst for change. Movements for justice and equality, from civil rights to gender equality, are rooted in the demand for respect and recognition of every individual's worth.

Quote for Reflection

"When we show respect for the rights of others, we sow the seeds of equality and peace." – Unknown

8. Building a Legacy of Respect

Respect is not just about the present—it creates a legacy for the future. By earning respect and teaching others to value it, we pave the way for a more compassionate, fair, and united world.

Final Pledge: A Commitment to Respect

"I pledge to treat others with respect, fairness, and kindness. I will strive to earn respect through my actions and integrity, and I will stand up for the dignity and rights of all people."

Conclusion

Respect is not a gift—it is an achievement. It is earned through empathy, integrity, and the consistent effort to uphold the dignity of oneself and others. As we conclude this journey, let us remember that respect is the cornerstone of human connection, the foundation of justice, and a vital tool for building a better world.

Chapter 11: A Call to Action

The journey to building a world where respect, dignity, and peace are the cornerstones of humanity is a shared responsibility. Every individual has a role to play in advocating for and protecting human rights. Whether through small, everyday acts of kindness or by supporting global movements, each of us can contribute to a brighter future.

This chapter provides practical steps readers can take to champion human rights both locally and globally. It also highlights organizations that are making a significant impact and deserve support.

How Readers Can Support Human Rights Locally and Globally

1. Educate Yourself and Others
Understanding the principles of human rights is the first step toward advocating for them. Read the Universal Declaration of Human Rights (UDHR) and familiarize yourself with its 30 articles. Share your knowledge with friends, family, and colleagues.

The Power of Respect

- Host a discussion group about human rights issues in your community.
- Use social media to raise awareness about global human rights challenges.

2. Advocate for Equality in Your Community

Change begins at home. Look for ways to promote equality and justice in your local community.

- Volunteer with organizations that support underserved populations.
- Advocate for policies that protect marginalized groups in your area.
- Report incidents of discrimination or injustice to the appropriate authorities.

3. Support Refugees and Displaced Communities

Refugees are among the most vulnerable populations, often forced to flee violence and persecution.

- Donate to organizations that provide food, shelter, and education for refugees.
- Volunteer at local refugee resettlement programs.
- Share stories that humanize the refugee experience and combat stereotypes.

4. Stand Against Discrimination
Whether it's based on race, gender, religion, or sexuality, discrimination erodes the foundation of human rights.
- Speak out when you witness discrimination or hate speech.
- Support anti-discrimination laws and initiatives in your community.
- Celebrate cultural diversity through events, art, and storytelling.

5. Support Fair Trade and Ethical Consumption
Every purchase you make is a vote for the kind of world you want to live in.
- Choose fair trade products that ensure workers are paid fair wages.
- Avoid companies that exploit labor or harm the environment.
- Support businesses owned by marginalized groups.

6. Donate or Fundraise
If you have financial resources, consider donating to human rights organizations. Fundraising is also a great way to involve others in supporting these causes.

- Host a fundraising event or campaign for an organization you believe in.
- Donate regularly to NGOs working on the front lines of human rights advocacy.

7. **Vote and Engage in Policy Advocacy**
   - Support leaders and policies that prioritize human rights.
   - Research candidates' stances on human rights issues before voting.
   - Write to your local representatives urging them to support human rights legislation.
   - Participate in peaceful protests and petitions to amplify your voice.

Organizations to Support
Here are some remarkable organizations making a global impact in the fight for human rights. Your support—whether through donations, volunteering, or advocacy—can help them continue their vital work.

1. **Amnesty International**
A global movement advocating for justice, freedom, and equality. Amnesty International investigates

human rights abuses and campaigns for the rights of marginalized groups worldwide.
Web https://www.amnesty.org

2. Human Rights Watch
This organization conducts research and advocacy to expose and combat human rights violations globally. Their reports bring international attention to injustices and hold governments accountable.
Web https://www.hrw.org

3. UNHCR – The UN Refugee Agency
The UNHCR provides life-saving assistance to refugees, including food, shelter, and medical care. They also work to find lasting solutions for displaced communities. Web https://www.unhcr.org

4. Save the Children
Focused on ensuring every child's right to survival, education, and protection, Save the Children works in over 100 countries to support children in crisis.
Web https://www.savethechildren.org

5. Equal Justice Initiative (EJI)
EJI fights for racial justice and provides legal assistance to individuals unfairly treated by the justice system, particularly in the United States.
Web https://www.eji.org

6. **The International Rescue Committee (IRC)**
The IRC provides aid to people whose lives have been shattered by conflict and disaster. They focus on health, education, and economic well-being for displaced families.
Web https://www.rescue.org

7. **Women for Women International**
This organization supports women in conflict zones, helping them rebuild their lives through vocational training, rights education, and community support.
Web https://www.womenforwomen.org

8. **Doctors Without Borders (Médecins Sans Frontières)**
Providing emergency medical care in war zones and disaster-stricken regions, this organization embodies the principle that health is a fundamental human right.
Web https://www.doctorswithoutborders.org

9. **Fair Trade Certified**
This organization works to ensure that farmers, workers, and artisans receive fair wages and safe working conditions.
Web https://www.fairtradecertified.org

10. **The Global Fund for Human Rights**
This fund supports grassroots organizations working to protect and advance human rights worldwide.
Web https://www.globalhumanrights.org

Respect in Action
Human rights are not just lofty ideals—they are the foundation of a just and peaceful world. But they cannot thrive without our collective action. Every effort, no matter how small, contributes to the global movement for equality, dignity, and respect.

As you close this book, I invite you to take the first step. Whether it's donating to an organization, educating a friend, or standing up against injustice, your actions matter. Together, we can build a world where human rights are not just protected but celebrated.

Respect is the bridge to peace. Let's walk that bridge together.

With love, hope, and respect.

Chapter 12: Reflections and Inspirations

Personal Reflections from My Journey

As I complete this book, my heart overflows with gratitude and resolve. Writing about the Universal Declaration of Human Rights (UDHR) has not only been an intellectual exercise but also a deeply personal journey. It has made me reflect on my life, the challenges I've faced, and the victories I've celebrated—both personal and shared with others around the world.

My journey has not been without struggle. I've faced moments of vulnerability, times when my own rights seemed precarious. From navigating personal adversities to advocating for justice in the face of opposition, these experiences have shaped who I am today. They've deepened my understanding of the importance of human rights, not as abstract ideals but as tangible protections that ensure dignity, fairness, and hope for all.

The Power of Respect

I vividly recall the times I turned to the principles of the UDHR for strength and guidance. Whether it was fighting for justice in legal battles or seeking to uplift the voices of the vulnerable, these universal rights served as a beacon, reminding me that even in the darkest moments, we are never truly alone.

My Instagram platform has been an outlet for these reflections. Through posts that celebrate equality, advocate for justice, and share stories of resilience, I've sought to inspire others to join the cause of human rights. Social media, while often criticized, has been a powerful tool for raising awareness, building solidarity, and amplifying voices that might otherwise go unheard.

Quotes That Resonate with the UDHR

As we consider the UDHR's timeless wisdom, it is important to draw inspiration from voices that echo its principles:

1. *"Our lives begin to end the day we become silent about things that matter."* — **Martin Luther King Jr.**

This quote reminds me of the importance of speaking out, no matter the odds. Silence in the face of injustice only perpetuates suffering.

The Power of Respect

2. *"Injustice anywhere is a threat to justice everywhere."* — **Martin Luther King Jr.**

This resonates with the UDHR's universality, affirming that human rights are interconnected and indivisible.

3. *"The future depends on what we do in the present."* — **Mahatma Gandhi**

Every step we take today to uphold human rights paves the way for a brighter, fairer tomorrow.

Instagram Highlights: Sharing the Message

One post that stands out is from my Instagram feed:

📸 "Freedom is our birthright. Justice is our demand. Together, we can create a world where every voice matters, every life is valued, and every right is upheld."

This caption accompanied an image of diverse hands holding a candle, symbolizing unity and hope. It resonated deeply with my followers, sparking a conversation about the power of collective action in advancing human rights.

The Power of Respect

Another post shared a personal moment of reflection: ☞ "This journey isn't about me—it's about us, about humanity. About the world we want to leave for our children. Let's make it one of peace, justice, and compassion."

These messages are more than captions—they're calls to action. They reflect my belief that change begins with awareness and grows through collaboration.

Inspiration from Activists and Everyday Heroes
Throughout this journey, I've drawn inspiration from activists like Malala Yousafzai, Greta Thunberg, and countless unnamed heroes who fight for justice daily. Their courage and resilience remind us that the UDHR is not just a document—it's a living, breathing testament to what humanity can achieve when we stand together.

Malala's fight for girls' education, Greta's relentless pursuit of climate justice, and the stories of refugees seeking safety remind us that human rights are not guaranteed. They must be defended, nurtured, and celebrated every day.

The Power of Respect

About the Author

Duchess Nivin El-Gamal is a multifaceted personality, renowned for her philanthropic endeavors, entrepreneurial spirit, and advocacy for humanitarian causes. As the Ambassador of Peace for the Universal Peace Federation (UPF-UN) since 2022 and Commonwealth Ambassador for the Commonwealth Entrepreneurs Club (CEC), she has solidified her position as a champion of peace, social justice, and human rights.

With a strong background in business, Duchess El-Gamal has successfully founded and managed several ventures, including the prestigious Duchess Prestige Cosmetics Brand, started in 2018. Her commitment to empowering others extends to her charity work, notably as the founder of SSAAMAC Charity, which provides vital support to war victims, natural disaster survivors, and children with MBL immune deficiencies.

Throughout her career, Duchess El-Gamal has received numerous accolades for her contributions to philanthropy, entrepreneurship, and humanitarian work. Her dedication to creating positive change has earned her recognition from esteemed organizations, including the Universal Peace Federation, the Commonwealth Entrepreneurs Club, Forbes, UCL, the Egyptian Culture Bureau, UK, Mother of the Year and multiple international organizations.

As a passionate advocate for child protection, health equity, and social justice, Duchess El-Gamal continues to inspire others through her remarkable journey, showcasing the power of resilience, compassion, and determination.

www.ingramcontent.com/pod-product-compliance
Ingram Content Group UK Ltd.
Pitfield, Milton Keynes, MK11 3LW, UK
UKHW020716260325
456749UK00005B/731